GETTING INTO YOUR WOK WITH ANNETTE ANNECHILD

GETTING INTO YOUR WOK WITH ANNETTE ANNECHILD

Learn How to Use Your Wok for Everything from Egg Making to Cake Baking!

PUBLISHED BY SIMON & SCHUSTER, NEW YORK

Cover photograph by Terry McKee
Line drawings by Karen Howitt

WALLABY BOOKS, A Simon & Schuster division of
GULF & WESTERN CORPORATION
1230 Avenue of the Americas, New York, N.Y. 10020

ISBN: 0-671-79137-0

First Wallaby printing Nov., 1980

10 9 8 7 6 5

Printed in the U.S.A.

Gently dedicated to
Leonora and Barbara Tint
and Brian M. Quill

You lit the candle . . .
it is with much love and appreciation
I now share the light.

Acknowledgments

Writing a book is creating a journey for the next few years of one's life. As it is born, it becomes the center of your existence. It is so much a part of you that it becomes part of those beside and all around you. Over the past few years, many people loved, shared, and helped me create this journal . . . I thank them now for their support, encouragement, and understanding. The time for celebration has come at last.

I'd like to extend a very special thank-you to Jerry and Cathy Laks for giving me the space and love in which to write this book; to Rick Bard, for guiding and selling it; to Gene Brissie, Joel Abel, Ron Busch, Milton Charles and all the people of Pocket Books for buying and building it; to the testers—Tamara Block, Jill Miller, Skip Skwarek, Rochelle Small, Barbara Tint, and my mother, Anne Viscardi—and all the contributors; to all the Tints for all the caring; to the Great White Whale Advertising Company for hiring a writer who doesn't type; to Penny of Pocomoke, and to Allen Balderson for his constant California energy; to Mary and Ralph Horky, Kathy Thiele, Russell Bennett, and Jonathan Elliott for being there for me in the crazy days of the final draft; to Linda Chambers for her fortitude, enthusiasm, and invaluable assistance throughout the project; to Empire Szechuan for keeping me alive when I was too tired to cook; to Woody Allen for keeping me laughing; and especially to Brian M. Quill, for sustaining the reality this fantasy survived in—I love you all.

A. Annechild

CONTENTS

3
Recipes

Getting Into Your Wok

Getting *You* into Your Wok . . . That's It! That's what this book is all about. It was written to let you know how simple and how much fun cooking in your wok can be.

It seems most wok cookbooks are either all about authentic Chinese cuisine or, at the other extreme, center around cutesy party recipes.

I have always felt the need for a book explaining the fundamentals of wok cookery in a simple way, integrating the premise of highly nutritious Oriental cookery with the American kitchen. You see, woks are great for eggs, vegetables, seafood, poultry, meat, stews, and desserts! They are inexpensive, easy to clean, and last forever. They have to be the most versatile everyday cookware in existence.

For me, it is the basic kitchen. With a wok and this cookbook, the most inexperienced cook can make a healthy and delicious breakfast, lunch, and dinner. Anything that good is worth knowing about. Just grab your wok and come along!

1
Making Friends with Your Wok

The first step in getting familiar with your wok is accepting and getting over the fact that it *looks* different. As with most things, the difference is surface and physical. You will find your wok to be as reliable, friendly, and forgiving as your favorite pot or pan.

After all . . . it is a pot *and* a pan. It fries, steams, boils, and poaches anything . . . and it is so easy to use and clean. Woks may be new to Americans, but remember—millions of people have been using them every day for centuries.

All of the steps are easy and practical. Just turn the page and . . .

. . . celebrate a whole new way of life with your wok! Feasting on lots of delicious fresh vegetables, seafood, and poultry, and going easy on the red meats, will make you look and feel terrific. This was not written to be a "dieters' cookbook," but by allowing Wokcookery to gradually improve your eating habits, you can be thin forever without ever mentioning the word "diet." If weight has been a problem for you, you'll be happy to note that the whole concept of Wokcookery is a thin idea! The recipes are basically all low-calorie—just go easy on the rice or try substituting a bed of bean sprouts. The reason dieting is so hard is because it's usually linked with the idea of deprivation.

In this book you will find ways of *indulging* yourself with health to let your body become the efficient machine it was created to be.

The premise of the book and of Wokcookery is to make food as beautiful to look at, as delicious to taste, and as beneficial to the body as possible. It encompasses my life experience with natural food, dieting, Oriental cookery, and an American-Italian heritage. It is a kind thing to prepare a meal for yourself or another human being. Your wok can help make it easy and fun. Enjoy!

Tips on Wok Buying

The recent surge of wok popularity in this country has brought with it an increased selection to choose from when buying a wok. Woks now come in aluminum, stainless steel, copper, brass, and iron. The best for heating evenly are rolled, tempered steel.

Woks range in size from 12 inches to 26 inches. For everyday home use, 14 inches to 16 inches is a good-sized selection. It will suit one and serve up to eight. For barbecuing, you might consider a larger size. It's great on the grill.

When shopping for a wok, pick the one that seems most convenient to *you*. Woks are available with one long wooden handle, as well as the traditional wok with two side handles. Some come in sets; if you do not buy a set, be sure to purchase the ring it will rest on over the burner (called the *dok*) and the cover. And remember, the best place to store your wok is right on top of the stove.

Utensils

Your wok may have come with a utensil set. If not, the basics can be purchased separately. For protecting the surface of your wok, I highly recommend the first three below—the other two are just nice to have. It's important not to use metal utensils because they will mar the surface.

1. The Bamboo Scrubber
   A must for cleaning—easy to use and gentle on the surface
2. Wire Mesh Strainer
   For lifting out foods when deep frying and skimming soups
3. The Flat Lifter
   Great for eggs and omelets—a must for seafood
4. The Ladle
   Like I said, nice to have, but your present ladle will work fine—just never scratch the surface with it
5. Chopsticks
   Great for stirring, but wooden spoons work too.

Wok Accessories

1. A chopping board is *absolutely essential,* as well as . . .
2. . . . a good, sharp knife or cleaver, and . . .
3. . . . a small, sharp utility knife.
4. An inexpensive wire whisk will come in really handy for all those sauces we'll make to top off delicious wokked delights!
5. A bamboo or metal steamer.
6. Any kind of little bowls to put sliced vegetables in when setting them aside. It will then be easier to add them.

Seasoning and Caring for Your Wok

Seasoning your wok is a most important first step, since it will prevent food from sticking to it. Here is an easy way to season a rolled steel, nonelectric wok:

1. Before using, wash it thoroughly. This is the one time Brillo can be used on your wok. Woks are packed in machine oil, which is important to remove.
2. Place wok on its ring (the dok) over burner.
3. Then fill it with hot water and boil for at least two hours over high heat. As it is boiling, continue adding water to the brim—otherwise a watermark will form below the edge.

4. Pour out water. Repeat the process if it seems necessary.
5. Dry it completely over burner over high heat, then turn off heat.
6. Next, with several thicknesses of paper toweling moistened with vegetable oil, rub the inside of the wok to close the pores. Repeat with fresh towels until the surface comes away clean. (Don't panic as you see black on the towels. It's not dirt—just the protective coating it is shipped in.)
7. When that's all off, you're ready to begin. If by chance your wok has special or different instructions for seasoning, simply follow them.

To clean wok after each use:

1. Wash with warm sudsy water, scrub with bamboo brush (available at all houseware stores) or nylon pad.
2. Place wok on dok over burner in upright position.
3. *Dry immediately over high heat.*
4. Let cool down and then rub lightly with 1 teaspoon of oil on a paper towel.

Be faithful in its care and you will be rewarded with a durable, well-seasoned wok.

Woks darken with use—that's part of their charm. They are cherished for their character and memories—you now own an heirloom!

Electric Woks need no seasoning since they are precoated with an easy-to-clean, nonstick surface.

2
Wokcookery: The Fun Part

The fun part is actually using it. Your wok has a quality I've never seen in a saucepan—it's exotic! After ten years of using one, I still get a tiny rush whipping up wokked scrambled eggs, and people respond—it's something new.

No matter how many woks are sold, a large number of them will, unfortunately, end up stored in their box instead of on top of the stove. Hence they will always be a sign of the gourmet adventurer. Once they've made it to the stove, however, they *rarely* get put away.

Okay, now *your* wok has made it out of the box, onto the stove, and has even been seasoned. You are now ready to become a Wokmaster!

The basic concept to understand is that most of the time spent in Wokcookery is in the *preparation of ingredients.* Everything must be ready *before* you begin heating the wok, for once you begin the cooking time is a matter of moments. So slice everything you will need and put it into individual little bowls. Have your oil and seasonings at hand. Then it's as easy as one, two, three.

The Basic Principle

One: Heat the wok over high heat.

Two: Once it is hot (2 to 3 minutes), make a necklace of oil around the top of the wok. It will slide down, coating the sides and leaving a little pool in the bottom.

Three: Immediately start adding ingredients and stir.

Congratulations—you've begun!

A Word About... HEAT

Wokcookery can be done over gas or electric heat. However, if you are using an electric stove you must be especially careful about temperature control. Instead of preheating your wok over high heat, use medium-high, since it will be impossible to quickly bring the heat down. The dok is designed for both gas and electric stoves. For gas stoves, place larger-diameter circle down; simply flip over for electric stoves.

Diagonal Slicing

Diagonal slicing is an Oriental tradition, and with good reason. By slicing with your knife at a 45-degree angle to the food, you produce thin slices that expose the largest possible area to heat, contributing to a fast cooking time. It is ideal in Wokcookery, since the cooking is done over high heat. Use this method for meats and fibrous vegetables and it will also help tenderize them.

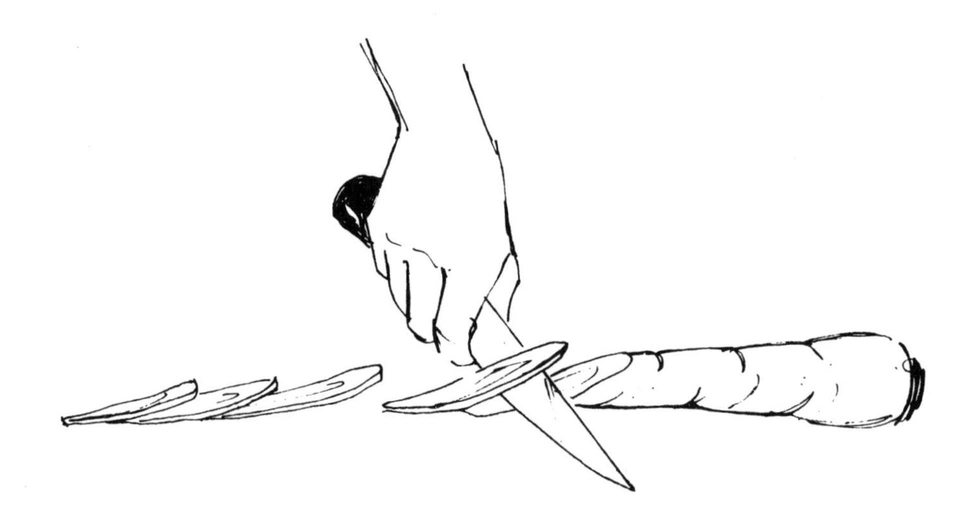

How to Like Cooking Better

A number one rule—clean as you go.

I know it sounds like something you've heard all your life, but it's true. Not having to face a destroyed kitchen after each meal can improve your attitude about cooking in general. Cleaning as you go makes the cleanup occur when you're in a high-energy, *before*-dinner mood.

Basic Methods of Wokcookery

1. *Stir frying* is exactly that. It's simply heating the wok, necklacing with oil, and tossing in the vegetables. Stir to coat with oil and keep stirring until vegetables are firm but tender. This method prevents loss of vitamins in water and never lets veggies get limp. The color of the vegetables will actually deepen and brighten beautifully.

2. *Steaming.* For three dollars you can turn your wok into a hassle-free steamer. A stainless steel insert can be purchased and fit right into your wok when you want to steam. You just boil water in the wok, put in the insert, lay your vegetables, fish, or whatever on top, and cover. I discovered a round cake rack also works fine, and you probably have one already. You can

also buy tiered wooden steamers that work well and can steam several dishes at once. Your wok may have come with two wooden crisscrossed sticks for steaming. They fit in the bottom and, again, you boil water beneath them in the wok and lay vegetables across in a heat-proof server. They work okay, but the three-dollar stainless steel type can't be beat. Steaming adds no calories and also loses no vitamins.

3. *Deep Frying.* A wok makes deep frying a pleasure rather than an ordeal. For many reasons, it is absolutely the perfect tool for the job.

It prevents spattering because of its shape and takes only 4 cups of oil (which is reusable) for a 14-inch to 16-inch wok. The intense and well-distributed heat seals the nutrients and flavors immediately into the food, assuring a light and especially delicate, nongreasy result. It also makes deep-fried food contain fewer calories, because there is no chance for the oil to be heavily absorbed.

Secrets of successful deep frying are to have the batter and food ice cold and the oil very hot (375° F., 191° C. on a deep-fat thermometer). Peanut oil is the best for deep frying since it will not smoke at this high temperature and also increases the nutritional value of the food.

4. *Poaching.* Poaching fish is an easy, fine-tasting method of preparation. It is especially good for the whole fish, but large thick fillets wrapped in a porous cloth will work well also. The wok's shape makes it ideal for poaching since the thickest part of the fish will be closest to the flame, allowing the whole fish to be cooked perfectly in the same amount of time.

To Poach Fish: Bring enough water to totally cover fish by 1 inch to boil in your wok. Then lower the heat so that the water is just below the boiling point, and place the fish in the wok. Cover and adjust the heat to lowest possible setting. Cook 10 minutes for a 12-inch fish, and lift out.

5. *Soup Making.* Because of its size and well-distributed heat, your wok is great for soups. However, if you are going to do a lot of soup making in the wok, I recommend your purchasing a second wok, for the long simmering process can

eventually break down the patina (or seasoned surface). With two woks you can keep one for soup making, poaching, steaming, and cake baking, and reserve the other for stir frying and egg making.

6. *Barbecuing.* Take your wok outside and on the road! It works great over a barbecue grill or hibachi. When camping, simply dig a fire pit and straddle the dok across it. Place the wok on the dok and you're all set.

7. *Cake Baking.* That's right, you can actually "bake" cakes in it—*steam* bake, that is. Starting on page *125*, a whole section on Wokcakery begins.

3
Recipes

Over the next pages you will find my favorites—everything from eggs to my mama's Italian spaghetti sauce. After you have gotten comfortable with the basic techniques, keep exploring. The possibilities are endless. You'll find many of your own favorite dishes completely adaptable to your wok.

A Word About Ingredients

As you read on you will find seeds—sesame, poppy, and caraway—used again and again in the recipes. The reason is that they are an interesting seasoning and are packed with protein. They can be found in your grocery store. With sesame, *unhulled* is always the best and cheapest. If you can't find them that way, however, a little can of hulled is worth trying for starters.

Scallions are known in some areas as spring onions or green onions.

And oils . . . The best for your body and your wok are the unprocessed, unfiltered ones. Sesame, peanut, safflower, and corn are my favorites for their light, delicious taste, and all the recipes use them interchangeably, unless otherwise specified. A great dispenser for oil is the squeeze bottle ketchup and mustard are often served in. One squeeze, and you can necklace your wok with ease!

Tamari

Tamari is the health food equivalent of soy sauce. It is even more delicious and lends the same salty flavor.

I have listed tamari as an ingredient in many recipes, so do try it if you can . . . however, it is always interchangeable with soy sauce.

I guarantee that any ingredients in the recipes that you are unfamiliar with are worth discovering. Most of the ingredients called for, however, are probably in your kitchen already or readily available in your area.

Brown Rice

Lots of wok recipes are especially good over brown rice. White rice tastes okay but does nothing but make you fat. Brown rice tastes better and is better for you. It is much higher in protein because nobody has stripped it to make it pretty. An easy way to have it on hand is to make a batch once or twice a week and always have it in the refrigerator. Using soup stock instead of water when preparing it will make it even more delicious and heathful. Rice keeps well in the refrigerator. It's not only great under many dishes but is great fried with vegetables for dinner or in the morning next to eggs instead of hash browns.

1. Put 4 cups water to boil.
2. Rinse 2⅓ cups brown rice with cool water. Drain.
3. Put 1 tablespoon oil in 2-quart pot. Heat over low flame.

4. Add rice and sauté till moisture is absorbed and rice smells nutty.
5. Add 4 cups boiling water to rice with 1 tablespoon tamari.
6. Do not stir. Allow to boil uncovered for 3 minutes.
7. Cover and cook over *low* heat for 45 minutes. Do *not* open or stir.
8. After 45 minutes, turn heat off but allow to sit unopened for 15 minutes.
9. Fluff with fork.
10. Serve. It will stay warm quite a long time and tastes great fried the next day.*

How to Read a Recipe

In these carefully tested, original recipes you will find all the ingredients listed first, followed by the preparation, which is written simply step by step. So just . . .

1. Read through the recipe to get a general idea of the preparation.
2. Check to make sure you have all the ingredients.
3. Put all the ingredients out and have them ready as listed.
4. Follow the numerically listed steps.
5. Enjoy the tasty rewards.

A beginner in the kitchen or an expert can meet with fun and success. If you've got any ideas about being a lousy cook, just forget them! Anyone can do it, and you're already on your way!

---

*Refrigerate loosely covered.

Yield

When you decide to make a recipe, one of the first things to figure out is how many people you are preparing for and how much the recipe yields as listed. It sounds simple enough, but if you've ever made a recipe that the author felt fed four and in reality fed only two of *your* hungry guests, you have an idea of what I'm talking about.

Everybody eats differently and has different notions of what it means to feed a family. In some families, one serving is all anyone ever wants—in others, two or three servings is commonplace. Now I happen to like food to be plentiful. You will find that wokked food is light, so you can eat more and it all keeps beautifully in the refrigerator for tasty leftovers. Therefore, I have chosen to write these recipes for *two hungry* people unless otherwise indicated. All of them can be easily adapted to your particular needs.

One-Wok Dinners

In this country we often think of dinner in terms of a green vegetable, perhaps a potato, and some type of either red meat, poultry, or fish. We even have paper plates designed with three separate sections for this very reason. Well, there is another dinner concept, which Orientals have enjoyed for years and has recently become more popular in this country. It's the one-dish dinner—a healthful combination of foods prepared together and very often served over rice or pasta. It is especially convenient and easy to cook this way, and the cleanup is a breeze.

Your wok is a master in this concept. It is large and strong, and it distributes heat evenly.

Just turn the page—a medley of delicious new dinner ideas awaits!

Poultry

Poultry is a great source of protein with few calories. It's used very often in Wokcookery. Most of the recipes will call for boneless, skinless breast of chicken* that will be cut into pieces. You can either buy it that way for convenience or buy it ribbed and remove it from the bone yourself for economy. Dark meat works well, too.

Here you'll find chicken in combinations with all different textures and tastes. Experiment and enjoy them all!

---

*A whole breast of chicken is in fact *both* sides of the chicken. In the following recipes I have listed both "whole," meaning both sides, plus "splits," meaning *one* of the two breasts.

The 1st STOP Peanut Chicken

On a warm Sunday in June, people drifting up Manhattan's Second Avenue had their senses titillated by the smell of stir-fried peanuts and chicken. This time it wasn't coming from a restaurant but a gourmet housewares shop—The 1st Stop Housewares, Inc.* They were holding Wokcookery's first demonstration. I was demonstrating basic stir-fry principles and came up with Peanut Chicken to help spread the word of the wonderful wok. One taste of Peanut Chicken and the realization of just how easy it is to prepare can make an instant believer out of anyone!

*1st STOP Housewares, Inc., 1025 Second Avenue near 54th Street, New York, New York 10022. (212) TE 8-0007. Open seven days a week.

The 1st  Peanut Chicken

INGREDIENTS:

- 2 raw boneless skinless chicken breast splits
- 2 scallions
- ½ pound fresh mushrooms or 1 8-ounce can
- 1 small head broccoli
- peanut oil for cooking
- 1 4-ounce package salted peanuts
- 2 tablespoons sesame seeds
- 2–3 tablespoons oyster sauce
- salt and pepper to taste
- hot cooked rice

1. Cut chicken into 1-inch strips. Set aside.
2. Wash and slice scallions. Set aside.
3. Wash and slice fresh mushrooms or drain canned. Set aside.
4. Wash broccoli, cut off thick stems, separate upper portion into flowerets. Slice the flowerets into thin lengthwise slices for fast cooking. Set aside.
5. Heat wok.
6. Necklace with oil.
7. Add peanuts. Stir fry 1 minute and remove.
8. Add pieces of chicken a few at a time, sprinkle with sesame seeds. Stir fry till chicken turns white, remove to a plate. Continue adding more pieces and sprinkling with seeds until all chicken has been stir fried and removed to plate.
9. Add broccoli, stir fry about 3 minutes.
10. Add scallions and mushrooms. Stir fry till vegetables are crisp and tender.
11. Put chicken and seeds back in wok and stir.
12. Add oyster sauce to taste and sprinkle with salt and pepper. Stir until chicken is tender.
13. Sprinkle with nuts.
14. Serve with rice.

Classic Poached Chicken

INGREDIENTS:

1 fryer (about 3½ pounds), cut up and rinsed
3 cups water or chicken stock (canned is fine)
1 bay leaf
¼ teaspoon dried ground chili peppers
½ teaspoon dried parsley or 1 tablespoon chopped fresh
½ cup tamari
1 teaspoon slivered fresh ginger (optional)
2 tablespoons flour
8–10 fresh sliced mushrooms
3 chopped scallions
1 minced clove garlic
3 tablespoons sesame seeds
hot cooked rice

1. Place chicken with water in wok, add bay leaf, chili peppers, and parsley. Cook until chicken is tender (about 30 min.).
2. Remove chicken.
3. Mix together tamari, ginger and flour, stir into boiling stock.
4. Cook over low heat, stirring steadily, until the boiling point.
5. Return chicken to wok, add mushrooms, scallions, garlic, and seeds. Cook 10 minutes covered.
6. Serve over rice.

Mr. Lee's Famous Chicken Special

I guess if there's anything my life has been, it's interesting. Maybe not secure or particularly well handled, mind you, but interesting—yes, *that* without a doubt! Mobility has been the key word. I've hopped from city to country, gone from one career to the next, and slid from one life-style into another. One of the more basic skills I have to thank for allowing me such freedom monetarily is waitressing. I've been the "Can I help you, sir?" lady from New York City to Chincoteaque Island. In this respect, New York City has it all over anywhere else. The restaurants in the Big Apple are definitely among the best in the world. One of these very special restaurants is Mr. Lee's Continental Cuisine on Third Avenue at 25th Street in Manhattan. Mr. and Mrs. Lee offer a marriage of the finest Oriental and French cuisine that is without equal. The excellent service there is provided exclusively by women—special women, by and large, who are working in the restaurant as well as on the individual dream that brought them to the city. One of them a while back was me.

It is with appreciation that I give you Mr. and Mrs. Lee's exquisite Chicken Special.

INGREDIENTS:

2 chicken breasts, boneless splits*
1 onion
½ pound snow peas (or one package frozen, defrosted)
¼ pound (Chinese, if possible) straw mushrooms
sesame oil for cooking
1 small can water chestnuts, drained
1 small can bamboo shoots, drained
salt and pepper to taste
2 tablespoons oyster sauce
2 tablespoons water
hot cooked rice

1. Cut chicken into pieces (about 2 inches in size). Set aside.
2. Cut onion in eighths. Set aside.
3. Wash snow peas, clip little stems. Set aside.
4. Wash mushrooms and slice. Set aside.
5. Heat wok.
6. Necklace with sesame oil.
7. Add chicken, sauté until chicken begins turning white and is approximately half-cooked.
8. Add onion and stir.
9. Add snow peas, mushrooms, chestnuts, shoots, salt and pepper, and keep stirring.
10. When vegetables are tender, add oyster sauce and 2 tablespoons water. Cover for 2 minutes.
11. Serve next to rice.

---

*For excellent variations, simply substitute thinly sliced veal or cubed beef for the chicken.

Chicken Cacciatore*

INGREDIENTS:

2 medium onions
1–2 green peppers
1 red pepper
3 cloves garlic
2 2-pound frying chickens, cut up
¼ cup olive oil
4 tomatoes
1½ cup tomato puree
¼ cup red wine
1½ teaspoon salt
⅛ teaspoon pepper
¼ teaspoon allspice (optional)
3 tablespoons tomato paste
1 teaspoon oregano
1 teaspoon basil
hot cooked rice or spinach noodles

1. Chop onions, green and red peppers. Set aside.
2. Mince garlic. Set aside.
3. Rinse chicken. Pat dry.
4. Heat oil in wok.
5. Brown chicken pieces a few at a time and then place on plate.
6. Add onions, peppers, garlic to oil and brown lightly.
7. Add remaining ingredients and bring to boil; simmer 10 minutes uncovered.
8. Put chicken back into sauce and simmer covered 15 to 20 minutes.
9. Take off cover and simmer 10 minutes more. Skim sauce for fat on surface.
10. Serve with rice or spinach noodles.

*Serves 4.

Cashew Chicken

This dish goes back to my earliest days in New York City with two very special ladies, Sandy and Deborah.

As aspiring actresses we all shared an apartment on East 22nd Street, and in between studying lines, discovering New York City, and struggling for the rent, we ate beautiful dinners together. It was a very unique alternate family for all of us. Cashew Chicken is one of the proud products of that time.

INGREDIENTS:

- 2 boneless chicken breast splits
- ½ pound fresh mushrooms or 8-ounce can
- 4 scallions
- 1 4-ounce can water chestnuts
- ½ pound fresh Chinese snow peas or 2 packages frozen snow peas, partially thawed
- ¼ cup tamari
- 2 tablespoons cornstarch
- ½ teaspoon sugar
- ½ teaspoon salt
- peanut oil for cooking
- 1 4-ounce package cashews
- 1 teaspoon sesame seeds
- 1 cup chicken stock (canned is fine)
- hot cooked rice

1. Slice chicken breasts into ¼-inch-thick slices and then cut into 1-inch pieces. Set aside.
2. Wash and slice fresh mushrooms or drain and slice canned mushrooms. Set aside.
3. Wash scallions, slice white part into ¼-inch slices. Cut green part into 1-inch lengths, slash both ends several times, making small fans. Set aside.
4. Drain water chestnuts and slice. Set aside.
5. Wash snow peas. If fresh, remove ends and strings. If frozen, this will already be done.

6. Mix tamari with cornstarch, sugar, and salt. Set aside.
7. Heat wok and necklace with oil.
8. Add nuts. Stir 1 minute and remove.
9. Add more oil (about 2 tablespoons) and add chicken and seeds to wok. Stir fry till meat turns white.
10. Add peas and mushrooms, pour in stock, simmer 2 minutes.
11. Add water chestnuts.
12. Stir in tamari mixture and cook until sauce thickens, stirring constantly.
13. Simmer 1 minute, uncovered.
14. Add scallions, stir one minute, then sprinkle with nuts.
15. Serve over rice.

Pineapple Chicken*

INGREDIENTS:

2 whole raw boneless skinless chicken breasts
1 tablespoon cornstarch
2 teaspoons cold water
1 teaspoon salt
1 teaspoon tamari
2–3 stalks celery (to equal 1 cup)
2 scallions
¼ pound fresh snow peas or 1 package, frozen and defrosted
4 slices pineapple (canned in water)
4 tablespoons pineapple juice (from canned pineapple)
4 tablespoons oil for cooking
1 teaspoon sherry
⅓ teaspoon Season all (optional)
1 tablespoon honey
hot cooked rice

1. Cut chicken into approximately 3-inches-long, 1-inch-wide strips and marinate in mixture of cornstarch, cold water, salt, and tamari for ½ hour.
2. Wash and cut celery into diagonal slices. Set aside.
3. Wash and slice scallions into ¼-inch slices. Set aside.
4. Rinse snow peas if fresh, clip ends. Set aside.
5. Slice pineapple into wedges. Reserve 4 tablespoons liquid.
6. Heat wok and necklace with oil.
7. Stir fry chicken for 3 minutes in two separate batches. Then put all of it back into wok.
8. Add celery, snow peas, and scallions, and stir fry together until chicken is lightly browned and vegetables tender.
9. Meanwhile, mix together pineapple wedges, juice, sherry, Season all, and honey.
10. Pour over browned chicken and tender veggies.
11. Simmer until thoroughly heated.
12. Serve with rice.

---

*Serves 2 to 4.

Sesame Chicken

INGREDIENTS:

- 2 raw boneless, skinless chicken breast splits
- 3 stalks celery
- 1 carrot
- 1 cup peas, fresh or frozen and partially thawed
- 1 small onion
- ¼ pound fresh mushrooms or 1 4-ounce can button mushrooms
- 1 cup hot chicken broth (can be made easily with bouillon cube)
- 1 small green pepper
- oil for cooking
- 1 teaspoon salt
- ¼ teaspoon pepper
- 2 tablespoons tamari
- 1 teaspoon chopped fresh parsley or ½ teaspoon dried
- 2 teaspoons sesame seeds
- 1 tablespoon cornstarch
- 2 tablespoons water
- ½ cup blanched toasted almonds, slivered
- hot cooked rice

1. Cut chicken into approximately 3-inches-long, 1-inch-wide strips. Set aside.
2. Slice celery and carrot diagonally. Set aside.
3. Wash peas if fresh. Set aside.
4. Dice onion. Set aside.
5. Wash mushrooms if fresh and slice, or drain canned mushrooms. Set aside.
6. Prepare bouillon. Set aside.
7. Slice pepper thinly. Set aside.
8. Heat wok.
9. Necklace with oil.

10. Stir fry chicken 3 to 5 minutes, stirring constantly, till chicken begins to turn white.
11. Add salt, pepper, tamari, parsley, sesame seeds, carrot, celery, peas, onions, mushrooms, and pepper.
12. Stir fry 2 minutes, and stir in broth.
13. Cover and cook over low heat 5 minutes.
14. Mix together cornstarch and water, and stir into mixture till thickened.
15. Add almonds.
16. Stir and serve hot with rice.

Barbara's Favorite: Party Chicken and Lobster Marengo*

Ah. . . and now it's time to meet Barbara. You were introduced to her in the dedication and here she comes with her favorite recipe. We've spent a lot of the past year working and playing around the wok; we've experimented with simplicity and entertained with indulgence. Here's a really special, beautifully decadent recipe that is a party in itself.

INGREDIENTS:

½ pound fresh mushrooms or 1 8-ounce can
2 cloves garlic
1¼ cups chicken bouillon
3 ripe tomatoes
¼ cup oil for cooking
4 whole raw boneless chicken breasts, halved and skinned
¼ cup + 2 tablespoons sherry
2 tablespoons flour
1 tablespoon tomato paste
1 crushed bay leaf
1 tablespoon fresh or 1 teaspoon dried chopped chives
½ teaspoon salt
⅛ teaspoon pepper
2 10-ounce packages frozen lobster tails
hot cooked rice

1. Preheat oven to 350°F.
2. Wash and slice fresh mushrooms or drain canned mushrooms. Finely mince garlic. Set aside.
3. Prepare chicken bouillon, if using packaged or cubes
4. Core and quarter tomatoes. Set aside.
5. Heat ¼ cup oil in wok.

*Serves 4 to 6.

6. Sauté chicken breasts one at a time till light golden brown, and place pieces in a casserole dish. Add more oil while cooking if necessary.
7. Spoon 2 tablespoons sherry over chicken in casserole.
8. Cover with foil and bake in 300°F. oven 25 to 30 minutes or until tender. While chicken is in oven, proceed to step 9.
9. Remove all but 2 tablespoons oil from wok.
10. Add mushrooms and garlic and stir fry till tender.
11. Blend in flour.
12. Add chicken bouillon and ¼ cup sherry and simmer, stirring constantly till thickened.
13. Add tomato paste, bay leaf, chives, salt, and pepper.
14. Simmer slowly 15 minutes.
15. Meanwhile, cook lobster tails by package directions. Remove meat from shell and cut into bite-size pieces.
16. Add lobster meat to sauce along with tomatoes.
17. Simmer sauce 5 to 8 minutes until lobster and tomatoes are just heated through.
18. Serve chicken breasts in large platter topped with lobster sauce with rice on the side.

Seafood

Your wok will make it fun and easy to put a variety of great-tasting seafood on the table. These next pages are filled with new and interesting ideas for high-protein, low-calorie seafood delights.

Prepare yourself for a feast!

How to Choose Fresh Seafood

The fresher seafood is, the better, and there are several points to observe in its selection.

FISH

1. The eyes should be bulging their surfaces, bright and clear.
2. Gills should be reddish pink. They should be without slime or unnatural odor.
3. The flesh should cling close to the bones, firm and elastic to the touch. Pressed down, it should bounce back.
4. Scales should retain their brightly colored sheen and adhere tightly to the skin.
5. All fish has a characteristic odor, but fresh fish never has an objectionable odor.

SHELLFISH

1. Clams, mussels, and oysters are good only when alive, which is indicated by a tightly closed shell. Even slightly opened shells are not to be used.
2. Crabs and lobsters are easily identifiable by the lively movements of claws and head. They must be alive till the moment of cooking.
3. Prawns and shrimp are greenish in color and firm to the touch.
4. Bay and deep-sea scallops are marketed shucked and should have a firm, white appearance when absolutely fresh.

Sweet and Sour Sea Bass

INGREDIENTS:

- 1½–2 pounds sea bass
- 1 teaspoon salt
- 3 scallions
- 1 small carrot
- ¼ cup green pepper
- 2 slices ginger root (or to taste, ginger is hot!)
- 2 tablespoons tamari
- 3 tablespoons wine vinegar
- 3 tablespoons sugar
- ½ cup cold water
- 1 tablespoon cornstarch
- 1 quart oil for deep frying (preferably peanut oil)

1. Wash and dry bass inside and out. Make 4 diagonal cuts on each side of bass so seasonings will be absorbed.
2. Rub inside and outside of bass with 1 teaspoon salt and let stand 15 minutes.
3. Wash scallions. Slice into ¼-inch pieces. Set aside.
4. Wash carrot and pepper and slice in very thin diagonal slices. Set aside.
5. Slice ginger into very thin strips. Set aside.
6. Mix tamari, vinegar, sugar, cold water, and cornstarch. Set aside.
7. Heat 1 quart of oil in wok to about 375°F.
8. Deep fry bass for 5 to 8 minutes or until golden. Remove and place in deep platter.
9. Remove all but 1 tablespoon oil from wok.
10. Stir fry scallions, carrots, and peppers.
11. Add tamari mixture and bring to boil
12. Pour mixture over fish and serve.

Spring Street Natural Restaurant Mariscada*

My first Friday night in New York City was filled with the realization that I was in the entertainment capital of the world and had absolutely no idea of where to go. I was living at a women's residence and, over the almost inedible food at dinner, turned to a new friend named Heather and asked if she was up for an adventure. I wanted to see something of the New York City nightlife and figured a restaurant was a nice, tame way to begin. But first we had to find a restaurant. I opened my treasured *Village Voice* and saw a little ad for a restaurant called Spring Street Natural. It felt right. It took us two hours to get there via a maze of unfamiliar buses and subways, but we did arrive, and it was absolutely worth the journey. We dined on tempura and rice, wine, and luscious desserts. The place itself was perfect for me. Classical music, wood, plants, and friendly people. It was the first of a hundred visits. It is still my favorite restaurant anywhere. Becoming quite a regular, I met the waitress of the year, beautiful Elaine; Steve, the quintessential bartender; and Robert, the creative man whose dream the restaurant was. As I suspected on my first visit, great people had created this great restaurant. Not least of all is Claudio, whose outrageously good recipe awaits you on the next page.

I thank them all for the countless great times and for sharing this special recipe with us here.

---

*Serves 6.

INGREDIENTS:

½ cup oil (olive and peanut combined)
1 clove garlic, minced
1 cup chopped scallions
¾ gram saffron
18 clams (scrubbed)
24 mussels (scrubbed)
2 leeks, chopped
3 cups mushrooms, sliced
2 tablespoons paprika
1 tablespoon pepper
3 tablespoons flour
3½ cups white wine
3–4 tablespoons Dijon mustard
¾ tablespoon salt
2 pounds shrimp (shelled) (if large, 16–20)
2 pounds bay scallops (rinsed)
hot cooked rice

1. Heat wok.
2. Necklace with oil.
3. Add garlic and scallions, and stir fry till golden.
4. Add saffron and stir.
5. Add clams and mussels, stir, and cover.
6. As shells begin to open, add leeks and mushrooms.
7. Add paprika and pepper.
8. Dust with flour.
9. Stir and add wine.
10. Add mustard and salt and stir.
11. Add scallops and shrimp. Stir fry till shrimp are pink, making sure there is enough sauce. If not, add more wine.
12. Simmer covered 3 to 5 minutes and serve with rice.

The Shrimp Garden

INGREDIENTS:

1 small green pepper
1 medium onion
2 tomatoes
1 small head cauliflower
1 pound shrimp in shell
2 cups plus 3 tablespoons water
oil for cooking
1–2 teaspoons fresh ginger, finely minced
1½ tablespoons arrowroot flour
salt and pepper to taste
hot cooked brown rice
tamari sauce

1. Wash green pepper and slice.
2. Peel and slice onion. Dice tomatoes.
3. Break cauliflower into flowerets and wash. Halve lengthwise if flowerets are large.
4. Shell shrimp, reserving shells. Place shells and 2 cups of water in a saucepan, cover, and bring to boil. Boil 15 minutes, strain stock and save. Discard shells.
5. Heat wok.
6. Necklace with oil.
7. Add onions, peppers, cauliflower and ginger. Stir fry about 4 to 5 minutes.
8. Add stock (from shells) and simmer till veggies are crisp and tender—about 5 minutes.
9. Add shrimp and cook till shrimp turns pink—about 5 minutes.
10. Dissolve arrowroot in remaining 3 tablespoons of water and add to wok.
11. Stir until mixture thickens, season with salt and pepper to taste. Stir in diced tomatoes and heat through.
12. Serve over hot brown rice, with tamari on the side.

Linda's Baby Clam Appetizer

This baby clam appetizer is the creation of a brand-new Wokmaster. Before Linda Chambers began working as my assistant on this book, she had never *seen* a wok and considered herself a "lousy cook." Well, working all those long hours got her hungry and typing the whole book twice got her interested.

Linda got started and has now traded her "lousy cook" title for that of Wokmaster! Nibble on her wonderful baby clams.

INGREDIENTS:

- 1 can (large) baby clams
- 2 medium green peppers
- 4 large fresh mushrooms
- 1/3 cup oil for cooking
- 1/3 cup Italian bread crumbs
- ¼ teaspoon onion salt
- 4 fresh Romaine lettuce leaves

1. Drain baby clams. Set aside.
2. Wash and slice peppers and mushrooms. Set aside.
3. Heat oil in wok.
4. Stir fry peppers and mushrooms till tender.
5. Add ¼ cup of bread crumbs to oil in wok. Set rest aside. Stir till bread crumbs are well moistened and peppers and mushrooms are coated.
6. Add clams. Stir.
7. Add remaining bread crumbs. Stir.
8. Sprinkle with onion salt.
9. Remove from heat and serve on lettuce leaves.

Sizzling Fish Strips*

INGREDIENTS:

1 pound flounder fillets
3 tablespoons tamari
4 tablespoons sherry
1 tablespoon sugar
¼ teaspoon salt
4 slices fresh ginger root, chopped finely
2 scallions, cut into ¼-inch pieces
1 tablespoon sesame seeds
2 cups oil

1. Cut the fillets into 1-inch strips.
2. Marinate 1 to 2 hours in tamari, sherry, sugar, salt, ginger, scallions, and sesame seeds.
3. Remove, pat dry, reserve liquid.
4. Heat oil in wok.
5. Meanwhile, heat marinade in saucepan, almost to boiling, lower flame, and keep hot.
6. Deep fry pieces of fish 2 to 3 minutes till golden. Do a few at a time to keep oil hot.
7. Spread on paper towel to drain.
8. Put the marinade in a bowl and use as a dip for the fish at the table.

---

*Great over brown rice!

Leonard's Favorite: Perfect Shrimp Fried Rice

If fried rice was going to be even mentioned here, my friend, director Leonard Peters, had to be a part of it. You see, Leonard *loves* fried rice . . . I mean, *loves* it! Chicken fried rice, pork fried rice, shrimp fried rice—it doesn't matter. *Any* kind of fried rice is his favorite. I bet he's had fried rice at practically every restaurant that serves it in New York City. He helped create this recipe and assures me it is one of the best he's ever tasted. Prepare with confidence . . . Perfect Shrimp Fried Rice.

INGREDIENTS:

7 mushrooms
3 scallions
4 tablespoons oil (approximately)
1 teaspoon sesame seeds
1 cup raw shrimp (cleaned)
optional: a dash of ginger powder or a grate of fresh ginger, and ¼ cup bean sprouts
4 cups *cold* boiled rice (works best with rice made the day before and refrigerated)
2 eggs, beaten
2–3 tablespoons tamari

1. Wash and slice mushrooms and scallions. Put into separate bowls. Set aside.
2. Heat wok.
3. Necklace with oil (about 3 tablespoons).
4. Add seeds and shrimp. Stir fry 3 minutes or till shrimp are pink.
5. Remove from wok. Set aside.
6. Add scallions. Stir fry.
7. Then add mushrooms (and bean sprouts and ginger, if using). Stir fry.
8. Add 1 to 2 tablespoons oil and add rice. Stir quickly and immediately with chopsticks to coat with oil.

9. Lower flame a little and keep stirring so rice doesn't stick.
10. Make a little well in rice with a spoon. Add eggs. Stir through.
11. Add shrimp to wok.
12. Add tamari.
13. Stir fry and serve hot with additional tamari.

This recipe can be easily varied by adding cooked ham or shredded pork at the end instead of shrimp or by substituting the shrimp with pieces of raw chicken, stir frying it in Step 4 with seeds till it turns white, and then removing it until Step 11.

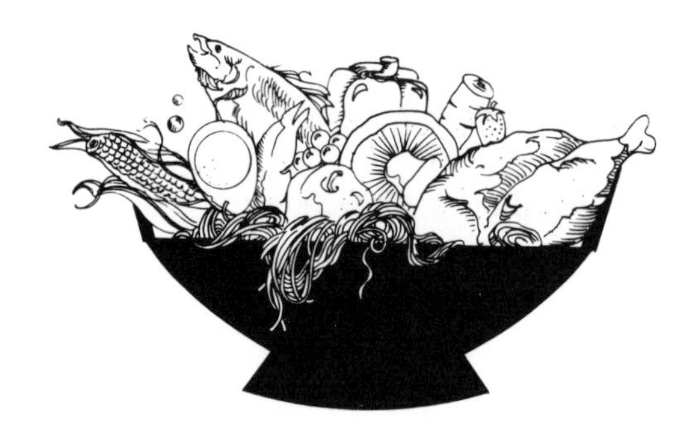

Nutty Oyster Fritters*

INGREDIENTS:

1–2 scallions
¼ cup macadamia nuts or almonds
2 egg yolks
1 8-ounce can chopped oysters
¼ teaspoon pepper
½ teaspoon salt
1 tablespoon fresh chopped parsley
1 teaspoon sesame seeds
¼ cup flour
2 egg whites
3 cups oil for frying
mustard

1. Mince scallions. Set aside.
2. Finely chop nuts. Set aside.
3. Beat yolks, add scallions, pepper, salt, nuts, parsley, and seeds. Combine, then sprinkle flour in and mix.
4. Beat egg whites till stiff (but not dry) and fold into yolk mixture along with oysters. Refrigerate batter.
5. Heat oil to 370° F. in wok.
6. Drop mixture in by the tablespoon and fry until browned on all sides.
7. Drain on paper towels.
8. Serve hot with mustard.

---

*Makes about 36 fritters.

Apple Shrimp Curry*

My friend, Michael, is somewhat responsible for this book's existence. Walking down West 85th Street one day, he casually suggested I combine my writing with my love of cooking. In the next moment I had decided on a project that was to encompass the next two years of my life. I've loved and hated him for it ever since, depending on the progress I was making. Well, I'm really thankful to him now, and in honor of him and his love of fine curry I created this next one.

INGREDIENTS:

1 medium onion
1 medium apple
¼ lemon
1 clove garlic
1 cup chicken bouillon
oil for cooking
2 pounds fresh shelled shrimp
2 tablespoons flour
1 cup light cream
2–4 teaspoons curry powder
1 teaspoon salt
hot cooked brown rice
condiments

1. Chop onion, apple, and lemon (without rind). Set aside.
2. Mince garlic. Set aside.
3. Prepare bouillon.
4. Heat wok.
5. Necklace with oil. Stir fry shrimp 1 pound at a time, 3 to 5 minutes, and remove.
6. Add onion, apple, lemon, and garlic.

---

*Serves 4.

7. Cook over low heat just until apple and onion are tender.
8. Stir in flour until smooth.
9. Add bouillon, cream, curry, and salt.
10. Stir over low heat until bubbly.
11. Add shrimp. Heat until warmed.
12. Serve over rice with condiments—coconut, cashews, chutney. Sprouts, shredded carrots, and peanuts are interesting to try, too.

Sesame Fish and Shrimp Balls*

INGREDIENTS:

½ pound shrimp, cleaned and minced
½ pound filleted fish, minced
3 scallions, minced
1 teaspoon sesame seeds
2 eggs (one for batter, one for dipping)
⅛ teaspoon salt
dash of flour
1 tablespoon fresh chopped parsley
3 cups oil
dip**

1. Beat all ingredients into a batter, except for 1 egg.
2. Roll batter into balls about 1 inch in diameter and refrigerate 1 hour on cookie sheet.
3. Dip balls into one beaten egg.
4. Heat 3 cups oil in wok.
5. Drop balls a few at a time into hot oil. (Be careful of splattering oil.)
6. Deep fry till brown. Keep warm in oven on wire rack in pan. Drain in paper towels. Serve with dip.

**DIP: Combine ¼ cup tamari, ¼ cup water, 1 finely chopped scallion, 2 slices ginger, finely minced. Refrigerate.

*Makes 24 to 30.

Maryland Crab Cakes*

Virginia may be for lovers, but Maryland is clearly for crabs! Living in Maryland, one adapts to the rather unpoetic slogan quite easily, for the crabs are outrageously good. Summer evenings there are filled with ice-cold beer and hot steamed crabs. Maryland is also recognized as having the tastiest crab cakes to be found on either side of the Mason—Dixon Line. Try them!

INGREDIENTS:

2 slices wheat bread
¼ cup milk
1 pound crab meat (Backfin is best)
1 teaspoon chopped parsley (fresh)
1 teaspoon sesame seeds
1 egg
1 tablespoon mayonnaise
1 tablespoon french mustard (Dijon is great!)
1 teaspoon Worcestershire sauce
salt and pepper to taste
1 cup oil for cooking
garnish: paprika, parsley, and lemon

1. Dip bread in milk and break into small pieces. Set aside.
2. Place crab meat in bowl and go through with fingers to remove shell.
3. Chop parsley. Set aside.
4. Add all ingredients (except oil) to crab meat and mix with your hands.
5. Heat 1 cup oil in wok.

*Makes 6 crab cakes.

6. Form batter into 6 patties.
7. Fry till golden, one at a time, on both sides.
8. Remove and keep in a warm oven on a wire rack placed in a baking pan so they will drain and stay hot.
9. To serve, arrange on platter, sprinkle centers with paprika, garnish with parsley and lemon.

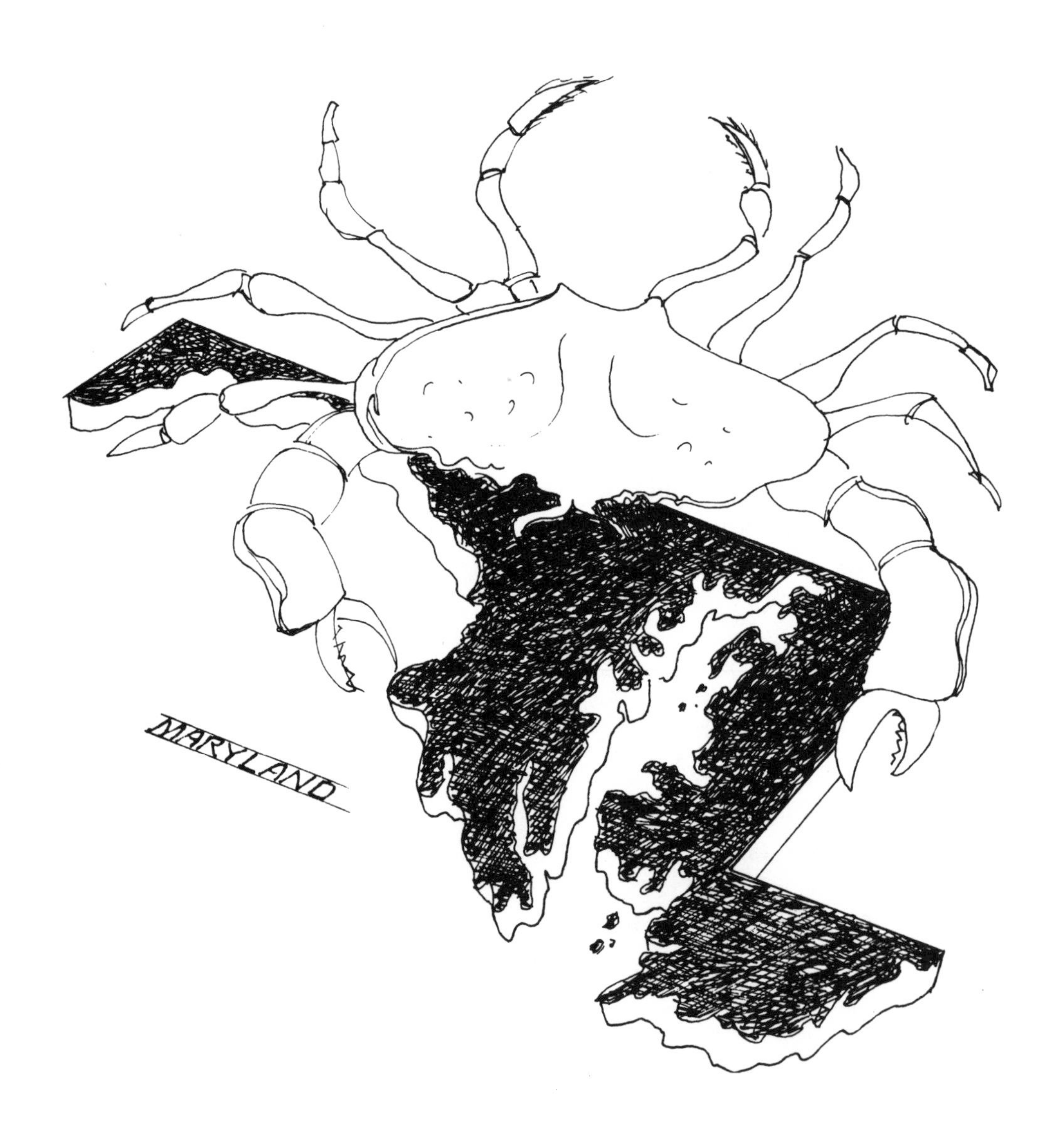

Salmon Patties*

INGREDIENTS:

1 can (15–16-ounces) pink salmon
1 egg
1 small onion, minced
1 tablespoon fresh chopped parsley
½ teaspoon dried dill
½ cup flour
1½ teaspoons baking powder
3 cups oil for cooking
tartar sauce

1. Drain salmon. Set aside 2 tablespoons juice.
2. In mixing bowl, mix salmon, egg, onion, parsley, and dill until sticky.
3. Stir in flour.
4. Add baking powder to salmon juice, stir, and add to salmon mixture.
5. Form into patties. Refrigerate about 1 hour.
6. Heat oil in wok to 370° F.
7. Deep fry patties for about 5 minutes, or until golden on all sides.
8. Serve with tartar sauce.

*Makes 6 patties.

Daddy's Recipe for Fish Fillets

(for the one that *didn't* get away)

Some say it takes a great fisherman to come up with a really great fish recipe, and they may well be right. My dad loves fishing and heartily enjoys the tasty rewards. He wouldn't think of masking the delicate taste of fresh fish with any overpowering ingredient. The following recipe is created especially to enhance the delicious natural flavor. Here your wok steps out as a steamer for a quick and tasty seafood delight.

INGREDIENTS:

- 1 tablespoon fresh chopped parsley
- 1 thinly sliced lemon
- 1 cup wine (white)
- 1 pound fresh fillets or thawed frozen fillets
- 1 teaspoon Jane's Krazy Mixed-Up Salt (or ½ teaspoon salt and ½ teaspoon Season all)
- ½ teaspoon Old Bay Seasoning (if you can get it)
- 1 tablespoon mayonnaise
- ⅛ teaspoon oregano
- ⅛ teaspoon pepper
- 1 tablespoon bread crumbs
- 2 tablespoons butter

1. Chop parsley and set aside.
2. Slice lemon into thin slices. Set aside.
3. Pour 1 cup wine into wok and simmer.
4. Place fish on steam rack, just above wine. (A cake-cooling rack works fine.)
5. Sprinkle on Jane's Krazy Mixed-Up Salt and Old Bay Seasoning.
6. Brush with mayonnaise.
7. Sprinkle parsley, oregano, pepper, and bread crumbs.
8. Dot with butter.
9. Lay thin lemon slices on fillets.
10. Cover and steam 20 minutes or until fish flakes easily with fork.

Leonora's Favorite: Seafood Fiesta

Leonora herself is a fiesta . . . a true fiesta of color, imagination, excitement, and warmth. The original version of this *Book of Wokcookery* was written for her on a memo pad one Saturday afternoon.

I had told her a lot about woks, and she decided to buy one. Wanting to make sure she "got into it," I offered to put together a few recipes. What was going to be a few handwritten pages became so much fun I began making it into a little booklet. It was a long Saturday, so I decided to put it into a little index card notebook with some drawings to go along with the recipes.

Well, Leonora really liked it—so much so she showed it to Ellen, a friend of hers who happens to be a literary agent. Ellen suggested it might actually work as a book. With much excitement, and a push from Michael Vines to combine my cooking with my writing, I embarked on the venture. There was the initial thrill of the first draft, then the monstrous rewrite. Many moons later, what you have in your hands became a reality I could hold in mine.

I created this recipe especially for Leonora, in honor of her ongoing fiesta of life. Celebrate with it!

INGREDIENTS:

¼ cup oil for cooking
1 teaspoon sesame seeds
1 clove garlic, minced
3 scallions, chopped
½ green pepper, sliced
1 carrot, sliced very thinly
1 14½-ounce can whole tomatoes drained (save liquid to use as part of water or stock)
1 6-ounce can tomato paste
3 cups water or stock
3 tablespoons Worcestershire sauce
2 teaspoons salt
1 bay leaf
1 tablespoon fresh chopped parsley or 1 tablespoon dried
½ teaspoon chili powder
½ teaspoon crushed basil leaves
½ pound crab meat
½ pound raw shrimp, shelled and deveined
1 pound flounder or sole, cut in chunks
¼ pound snow peas fresh or 1 package partially thawed
hot cooked rice

1. Wash, slice, and arrange all ingredients.
2. Heat oil in wok.
3. Stir fry seeds, garlic, scallions, green pepper, and carrot.
4. Add tomatoes, paste, stock or water, Worcestershire, salt, bay leaf, parsley, chili powder, and basil. Simmer uncovered 30 minutes. Remove bay leaf.
5. Add crab, shrimp, flounder or sole, and snow peas. Stir.
6. Simmer 10 to 12 minutes. Serve in bowls over rice.

Meats

Eating a lot of meat is not a very good idea. It is hard to digest and high in cholesterol and calories. Many people feel, however, that some meat is very important to their diet, so I have included the following meat recipes. It is much better to eat meat early in the day to give your body more time to digest it. Ideally, meat would be considered as the menu for special occasions rather than as part of a daily diet. You will find in wokcookery that meat is thinly sliced which will aid in digestion and also help stretch the food budget!

Flank Steak with Oyster Sauce

INGREDIENTS:

¾ pound flank steak
3 tablespoons bottled oyster sauce
1 tablespoon sherry (dry)
2 tablespoons peanut or corn oil

1. For easy slicing, freeze the steak (but not too solidly) and then slice into 1-inch-wide, ¼-inch-thick strips.
2. Mix oyster sauce and sherry in bowl. Set aside.
3. Heat wok.
4. Necklace with oil.
5. Add steak slices. Stir fry till desired doneness.
6. Stir in sauce mixture, and serve when sauce is thoroughly mixed with steak.

Lone Star Texas Bar-B-Q*

In January of 1977, Manhattan's first Texas-style nightclub opened its doors. It featured true Texas favorites on the menu and the music was strictly honky-tonk. Well, as it turns out, a lot of New Yorkers and out-of-town visitors really related to the taste and sound of the Lone Star State.

It was great fun working there, and I acquired a great big appetite for Lone Star cooking. After moving on, it was necessary to figure out how to make it myself when that special craving hit.

For the little bit of Texas in all of us . . . Lone Star Texas Bar-B-Q!

INGREDIENTS:

- 1 tablespoon onion
- 1 cup celery
- 1 cup green pepper
- 2 pounds ground beef
- 3 teaspoons vinegar
- 1½ cup ketchup
- 5 tablespoons water
- 2 teaspoons dry mustard
- 1 teaspoon salt
- ½ teaspoon chili powder
- fresh warm buns

1. Chop onion, celery, and green pepper. Set aside.
2. Brown beef in wok over medium heat.
3. Add onion, celery, pepper. Simmer till celery is soft.
4. Mix together vinegar, ketchup, water, sugar, dry mustard, salt, and chili powder.
5. Add to wok.
6. Simmer 10 minutes.
7. Serve over warm split buns.

---

*Serves 4.

Chinese Pepper Steak

Fresh ginger is purchased by the root. It is available at Chinese vegetable stands and possibly at your grocery store. You can also order it by mail or substitute ¼ teaspoon of ground ginger, which is readily available everywhere.

INGREDIENTS:

1 pound piece of round or sirloin of beef
¼ cup + 1 tablespoon tamari
1 tablespoon sugar
2 onions
2 green peppers
¼ cup of oil
1 clove garlic, minced
1-inch slice ginger root, chopped or 1½ teaspoon ground ginger
2 teaspoons cornstarch
hot cooked rice

1. Freeze the beef, not too solid, so that it will slice easily. Slice into thin strips.
2. Pour the tamari (¼ cup) and sugar over meat and marinate ½ hour.
3. Cut onions and peppers into wide wedges. Set aside.
4. Heat wok.
5. Necklace with oil.
6. Add garlic, stir fry till golden, and remove.
7. Add onion, pepper, and ginger. Stir fry 3 minutes.
8. Add meat with marinade and stir fry 3 minutes.
9. Blend the cornstarch and 1 tablespoon tamari. Add to wok.
10. Cook 15 to 20 minutes and serve on a bed of rice.

Cousin Ginny's Beef Stroganoff

The early years of my life were filled with the best of Italian cooking. My father being Sicilian and my mother being Neapolitan guaranteed relatives that were super in the kitchen. Aunt Mary and Uncle Freddie fed their children Ginny, Cookie and Paul (along with me!) delicious treats for years. Ginny grew up to live in the kitchen as much as I do, experimenting with every type of cooking. Next is her quick-and-easy Russian specialty, Beef Stroganoff.

INGREDIENTS:

1 pound round steak
1 onion
oil for cooking
1 clove garlic, minced
1 can cream of mushroom soup
½ cup sour cream
¼ cup water
2 cups egg noodles, cooked and drained
1 tablespoon chopped fresh parsley

1. Slice steak into thin strips.
2. Chop onion. Set aside.
3. Heat wok.
4. Necklace with oil.
5. Stir fry garlic, and then add and stir fry beef and onions until well browned.
6. Stir in soup, sour cream, and water.
7. Cook over low heat about 45 minutes.
8. Prepare noodles as directed.
9. Serve beef over hot noodles. Sprinkle with parsley as garnish.

Hungarian Goulash

INGREDIENTS:

1½–2 pounds beef cubes
flour seasoned with salt and pepper for dredging
oil for cooking
1 small onion, sliced
1 small pepper, sliced
1 cup boiling water
1 beef bouillon cube
1 bay leaf
8 ounces flat (medium or wide) noodles, cooked, drained, and buttered

1. Dredge beef cubes in flour. Set aside.
2. Heat wok.
3. Necklace with oil.
4. Brown peppers and onions till golden and remove.
5. Brown beef cubes quickly on all sides.
6. Combine water and bouillon cube in a cup.
7. Add to meat in wok.
8. Add onion, pepper, and bay leaf in wok.
9. Cover and simmer 1 hour or until meat is tender.
10. Serve over hot buttered noodles.

Skip's Sweet and Sour Pork*

Skip Skwarek came in right at the end of this project. I had just signed the book with Pocket Books and, after the initial ecstasy, soon developed a posture of sheer panic. I wanted to be sure the book was perfect and easy to follow for everybody. I met Skip in the midst of all this and found he was quite a chef in his own right, with a catering service called EATS! He came right in and went to work, helping test and perfect in the final days. He experimented with the Sweet and Sour recipe and I so liked the results that the recipe that follows must be credited as his very own. The part I liked best was *no sugar!* He experimented with honey and came up with a fabulous Sweet and Sour I'm sure you'll love.

I always think of sweet and sour as combining the best of both worlds. The sour takes the edge off the sweetness and the touch of sweet is there to round out the sour. It certainly transforms shrimp, pork, or vegetables into a distinct and different change-of-pace dinner idea.

This recipe can be altered with the same results by roasting the pork in the oven, allowing it to cool slightly, and then slicing it into 1-inch cubes. Then proceed from Step 7 on as directed.

---

*Serves 4.

INGREDIENTS:

1½–2 pounds boneless pork roast (preferably loin, but you can use shoulder)
oil for cooking
¾ cup vinegar
¾–1 cup honey (to taste)
6 tablespoons tamari
2 cloves garlic, minced
1 tablespoon freshly minced ginger
3 cups + 6 tablespoons water
3 tablespoons cornstarch
1 cucumber, peeled, seeded, and cut into 1-inch sticks
¾ pound bean sprouts
hot cooked rice

1. Cut meat into strips, ⅛-inch thick, 2 inches long.
2. Heat wok over medium heat.
3. Necklace with oil.
4. Add meat and stir fry until well browned on all sides.
5. Remove meat from wok. Set aside.
6. Empty oil from wok. Clean with paper towel.
7. Next combine vinegar, honey, tamari, garlic, and ginger with 3 cups water in wok.
8. Mix cornstarch and 6 tablespoons water to make paste.
9. Add to wok and cook, stirring constantly over medium heat until mixture is thick and smooth.
10. Add meat and cucumber to wok. Mix well.
11. When meat is thoroughly heated, stir in sprouts and serve over rice.

Chinese Liver, Onions, and Bean Sprouts

Liver is well known for its low price and high nutritional content. After trying this dish, it will be remembered for its fantastic taste. With a little imagination, liver can be exotic! And like most wok dishes, this one is low in calories—only 250 per serving. Enjoy!

INGREDIENTS:

- 4 small onions
- 1 pound baby beef liver
- ½ teaspoon ginger (finely minced if fresh)
- 3 tablespoons sherry
- sesame oil for cooking
- 1 pound bean sprouts, fresh if you can get them, canned and drained if you can't
- 3 tablespoons tamari

1. Slice up onions, set aside.
2. Cut liver into 1-inch pieces. Put into a bowl with ginger and wine. Toss lightly and marinate for 15 to 20 minutes.
3. Heat wok.
4. Necklace with oil.
5. Brown liver quickly.
6. Remove liver and add onions. Stir fry until transparent.
7. Add sprouts and tamari and stir over high heat.
8. Add liver and cook until hot and serve.

Carne Pizziole*

I'm an Italian who never looked like an Italian. Light hair and blue eyes are certainly no clue. As a matter of fact, the only real clue is in the kitchen. Bring on the tomatoes, the oregano, and the garlic, and I'm cooking up a storm! Well, Carne Pizziole is a very Italian way of preparing round steak. This is one Italian dish even calorie counters can enjoy . . . without a touch of cheese or a hint of pasta, it glorifies that zesty Italian flavor.

So, as my Grandmother Viscardi says, "*Mangia!*"

INGREDIENTS:

- olive oil for cooking
- 1 clove garlic, minced
- 1 tablespoon chopped fresh parsley or ½ teaspoon dry parsley
- 2 pounds thinly sliced round or top sirloin steak
- 1 2-pound 3-ounce can Italian peeled tomatoes**
- ⅛ teaspoon oregano
- ⅛ teaspoon salt
- pepper to taste
- 1 teaspoon sugar
- dash of wine
- 1 8-ounce can tomato sauce

1. Heat wok over medium heat.
2. Necklace with oil.
3. Brown garlic.
4. Add parsley and meat, brown, and remove.
5. Add tomatoes to wok.
6. Add seasonings and stir; lower heat.
7. Simmer ¾ hour.
8. Add can of sauce, simmer 5 minutes.
9. Return meat to wok and simmer together 15 minutes.
10. If calories aren't a consideration, serve with mashed potatoes, peas and garlic bread.

---

*Serves 4.

**Remove stems and pulp in tomatoes by hand or purée in blender for 2 seconds.

Cathy's Chili*

One day I realized almost everything I've ever read or been told has come from the mouths and minds of men. Being a woman, that's a little scary. I mean, I like men a lot, but to live in a female mind and body and constantly be influenced and judged by a male is a freaky thing! Well, thank God, the last few years have brought significant changes for women—not so much in terms of our acquiring equality, perhaps, but more so in defining and understanding it for and in ourselves. Nowhere were women treated less equally than by each other, and I think that is changing in our growing new awareness. We need each other more now than ever to live and work through the immense changes in our minds and in our lives. The need to compete with each other is being overcome by yet another need—the need to communicate. We are looking for and very much need to find our "wholeness." For the first time in my life, women are as important and special to me as men have always been. I've found there are some really incredible New Age ladies out there, and my friend Cathy Laks of Cathy's Chili is one of them.

We've shared our changes, our thoughts, and our time over the past five or so years as well as countless feasts. Let me tell you, there is *no* better chili than Cathy's Chili!

---

*Serves 4.

INGREDIENTS:

3 stalks celery
2 onions
5 mushrooms
1 28-ounce can tomatoes (whole, peeled)
1 10-ounce can tomato soup
1 small can tomato paste
1 15-ounce can dark red kidney beans
salt and pepper to taste
2–4 tablespoons chili powder
2 tablespoons parsley flakes
1 pound ground beef
1 pound rice or elbow macaroni, cooked
cheddar cheese (optional)
sour cream (optional)
chopped raw onion (optional)

1. Dice celery, peel and chop onions and wash and slice mushrooms. Set aside.
2. Heat wok.
3. Add tomatoes, soup, tomato paste, and kidney beans (drained).
4. Add salt and pepper to taste, chili powder, and parsley.
5. Let simmer, stirring occasionally to prevent sticking.
6. In large frying pan (or another wok, if you're that lucky!) stir fry celery, onions, and mushrooms.
7. Add to tomato mixture.
8. Brown meat in same pan and then drain off all fat before adding to tomato mixture.
9. Simmer for 1 or more hours.
10. Serve with rice or elbow macaroni. Top with chopped raw onion, shredded cheddar cheese, or sour cream.

Note: Combine leftover elbows or rice and chili and refrigerate; it's even better warmed up the second day!

Stews

The word *stew* for me evokes images of old, toasty-warm country kitchens and a mother hovering over the stove with a wooden spoon. The next generation might well picture Mom and Dad in a colorful modern kitchen, simmering the stew in a well-seasoned, cherished wok.

You'll believe it when you try it. Woks are great for stews. Simmer slowly over a low fire and the well-distributed heat will guarantee a tasty fare.

Scallop Stew*

INGREDIENTS:

3 potatoes
2 onions
2 stalks celery
1½ pounds bay or sea scallops (rinsed)
oil for cooking
1 tablespoon sesame seeds
1 teaspoon poppy seeds
2 cups water or stock
1 teaspoon salt
¼ teaspoon pepper
2 tablespoons chopped fresh parsley or 1 tablespoon dry
1 pint half-and-half
½ pound mushrooms, thinly sliced
1 teaspoon tarragon
1 tablespoon butter
hot cooked rice

1. Wash and dice potatoes. Set aside.
2. Chop onions and celery. Set aside.
3. Cut scallops into halves or quarters. Set aside.
4. Heat wok.
5. Necklace with oil.
6. Stir fry onions and celery and seeds.
7. Add potatoes and stock (or water) and cover.
8. Simmer 15 minutes. Add scallops, cover, and simmer 10 minutes.
9. Add salt, pepper, parsley, half-and-half, mushrooms, tarragon, butter, and heat through.
10. Serve immediately over rice.

---

*Serves 4.

Sicilian Seafood Stew*

INGREDIENTS:

2 cloves garlic
1½ pounds fish fillets
2 tablespoons olive oil
2 cups canned strained tomatoes
1 cup white wine
1 teaspoon sesame seeds
1 dozen clams
1 dozen mussels
½ pound shelled shrimp
½ pound bay or sea scallops
½ teaspoon salt
¼ teaspoon pepper
2 tablespoons fresh chopped parsley
½ teaspoon basil
hot cooked rice

1. Mince garlic. Set aside.
2. Cut fish fillets into pieces.
3. Heat wok.
4. Necklace with oil.
5. Add garlic, tomatoes, wine, seeds, and bring to boil.
6. Simmer uncovered 5 minutes.
7. Add all seafood and seasonings and baste.
8. Simmer covered 10 to 15 minutes until clams and mussels open and shrimp are pink.
9. Serve over rice.

*Serves 4.

Russell's Cuban Black Bean Stew*

I will always remember Russell as something of a savior. He absolutely got me through my first night as a waitress. Of course, I had lied to get the job ("Who, me? Of course! *Tons* of experience! *Tons!*"). I showed up on the first night, found out how much money they were making, and was instantly determined to keep the job. Halfway through the rush, I quietly confessed to Russell that I had *never* been a waitress before, could barely count as high as the number of people at my station, and had absolutely no idea what to do. He then uttered three words that have stuck in my head ever since: "Just don't freak." He was right . . . that was *it!* Smile, look confident, keep moving, and everything'll somehow work out all right. He did me a great service. He also taught me how to give *other* people really good service, and even how to have fun while doing it.

The book would have been incomplete without his touch. He has his own excellent and exciting catering service now, "BEFORES"**—quite a chef he's become. I thank him for his offering, taken from his own personal and private archives.

---

*Serves 4 to 6.
**"BEFORES"
finger foods for feasting
Russell Bennett
(212) 989-0358

INGREDIENTS:

2 cloves garlic
2 medium-size onions
1 pound canned or fresh tomatoes
oil for cooking
½ pound bacon or pork fat
1 package black beans (soaked overnight)
2 medium-size bay leaves
½ cup dried parsley
1 teaspoon cayenne pepper
water

1. Mince garlic. Set aside.
2. Chop onions and tomatoes. Set aside.
3. Heat wok.
4. Necklace with oil.
5. Stir fry pork, garlic, onions for 3 minutes. Add all the other ingredients. Cover with water to 1 inch over surface.
6. Simmer 3 hours and serve.

Burgundy Beef

INGREDIENTS:

¼ pound salt pork (cubed)
1¼ pounds beef for stew (cubes)
2 whole onions stuck with 6 cloves
2 carrots, quartered
1 bay leaf
1 pinch thyme
1 sprig parsley
salt and pepper to taste
1 bottle dry red wine
oil for cooking
2 tablespoons flour

1. Marinate all ingredients except oil and flour together for 12 hours.
2. Remove meat and onions.
3. Heat wok.
4. Necklace with oil.
5. Add meat and onions and brown.
6. Thicken with flour.
7. Add marinade.
8. Cook slowly for 3 hours and serve.

Lamb Stew*

INGREDIENTS:

4 potatoes
4 carrots
2 white turnips
1 cup fresh or frozen peas
3 tomatoes
2 pounds lamb cubes (shank, breast, neck or shoulder), cut into bite-size pieces
flour for dredging
oil for cooking
salt and pepper to taste
hot water

1. Wash and cube potatoes. Set aside.
2. Wash and cut carrots in thick diagonal slices. Set aside.
3. Wash and slice turnips. Set aside.
4. Wash peas. Set aside.
5. Cut up tomatoes into wedges. Set aside.
6. Dredge lamb with flour. Set aside.
7. Heat wok, necklace with oil.
8. Brown lamb well, adding oil as necessary.
9. Season with salt and pepper and cover with hot water, simmering till nearly tender (about 1 hour).
10. Add all veggies except tomatoes and simmer 30 minutes longer or until crisp and tender.
11. Add tomatoes, heat through, and serve.

*Serves 4.

Shepherd's Pie

A delicious, old-fashioned use of any leftover stew.

Line baking dish with hot mashed potatoes. Fill center with hot stew, cover with additional mashed potatoes, and place in hot oven (425°F.) for 15 minutes until potatoes are browned. browned.

VEGETABLES

In the old days everyone thought of vegetables as limp, on the side of the plate, either frozen or canned, and *always* tasteless. A lot of us grew up then. Welcome to the New Age!

We now realize vegetables are alive and well and should live close to our hearts. When properly prepared they are absolutely beautiful and taste yummy.

Lucky you! Your wok is the perfect place for preparing them.

The basic principle here is "Save the vitamins!" Additional water destroys vitamin content—so either steam or stir fry. They should be crisp and colorful when served. Also, *only peel vegetables when absolutely necessary,* since an enormous amount of vitamins are stored in the skin. Don't be surprised if what started out stuck in the corner of the plate takes front and center! Delicious veggies have a habit of working their way into the main course.

A Side

It's hard for me to ever call a vegetable a side dish, because fairly often I'll eat a head of broccoli or cauliflower as a main meal. However, I am known to be pretty eccentric at times, so . . . the following recipes are one- or two-vegetable dishes that you would probably serve as a partner to something else for dinner or as a nice, hot lunch.

Sidecar Broccoli and Cheese

INGREDIENTS:

1 head broccoli
1 scallion
1 clove fresh garlic
oil for cooking
2 tablespoons sesame seeds
salt and pepper to taste
2 slices Muenster cheese* (cut into 2-inch-wide strips)

1. Rinse broccoli with cold water after breaking into flowerets. If flowerets are large, slice vertically. Set aside.
2. Chop scallion into small pieces. Set aside.
3. Mince garlic. Set aside.
4. Heat wok.
5. Necklace with oil.
6. Add seeds and garlic and stir fry till golden.
7. Add scallion and stir.
8. Add broccoli and toss.
9. Stir fry until crisp and tender.
10. Add salt and pepper and toss.
11. Lay strips of cheese across top, sprinkle sides of wok with cold water, and cover tightly to create steam.
12. Ready when cheese is melted!

---

*For a variation, substitute either Swiss cheese or ½ cup of Parmesan cheese.

Queen Cauliflower

INGREDIENTS:

1 large cauliflower or 2 packages frozen, thawed
2 onions
2 cloves garlic
¼ cup oil for cooking
1 teaspoon sesame seeds
2 cups whole tomatoes in puree (canned)
1½ teaspoons salt
½ teaspoon black pepper
½ teaspoon basil
¼ teaspoon oregano
a splash of wine
¼ cup chopped parsley
optional: grated Parmesan cheese on top

1. Wash cauliflower, break into flowerets, and set aside.
2. Slice onions. Set aside.
3. Mince garlic. Set aside.
4. Heat wok.
5. Necklace with oil.
6. Add onions and seeds. Stir fry till golden.
7. Add garlic, tomatoes, salt, pepper, basil, oregano, and wine.
8. Bring to boil. Cook over low heat 10 minutes.
9. Add cauliflower.
10. Cook fresh cauliflower 20 minutes, frozen 10 minutes.
11. Sprinkle with parsley and serve.

The Careys' Colorful Side Dish

This one's as beautiful to look at as it is delicious to eat!

INGREDIENTS:

an equal amount of carrots, onions, and red beets
sesame oil for cooking
1 teaspoon sesame seeds

1. Cut onion into strips. Set aside.
2. Cut carrots thinly on a diagonal. Set aside.
3. Cut red beets julienne or into other interesting shapes. Set aside.
4. Heat wok.
5. Necklace with oil.
6. Add carrots and beets. Stir fry 5 minutes or until almost tender.
7. Add onions and stir fry to almost desired doneness.
8. Sprinkle with sesame seeds and stir one minute over heat then serve.

Cabbage Is for Kings

A member of the mustard family, cabbage has been cultivated for more than 4,000 years and is the most ancient of all vegetables. It has an aristocratic history dating back to the pharaohs. They ate large quantities of it before drinking bouts on the premise that they could guzzle more without getting drunk. The Egyptians actually went so far as to worship the vegetable as a god and build altars for it. The Greeks claimed that the heads "sprang from the sweat of Jupiter," recommending them as a cure for baldness and many other ailments, and the Romans saw cabbage as an aphrodisiac. Brought to the Americas by French navigator Jacques Cartier in 1536, cabbage has been cultivated here ever since. In this country, however, its aristocratic history has been forgotten, and the vegetable is not considered as special as it really is.

Cabbage is full of niacin, a building block in nutrition, and costs only pennies to serve. There aren't too many deals like this left, so be sure to check out fresh cabbage—a royal treat to be sure! This preparation is easy and delicious.

INGREDIENTS:

1 head cabbage
oil (sesame is especially good here)
salt and pepper to taste
2 tablespoons butter
1 teaspoon caraway seeds
2 tablespoons tamari

1. Cut cabbage into 1-inch strips and rinse with cool water.
2. Heat wok.
3. Necklace with oil.
4. Toss in cabbage and stir fry.
5. Season with salt and pepper; add butter, caraway seeds.
6. Sprinkle with tamari and stir.
7. Cook only until tender.
8. Serve with additional tamari.

Sweet and Sour Red Cabbage

If you enjoy Sweet and Sour Shrimp or Pork, be sure to try the spectacular flavor of sweet and sour designed this time for red cabbage. Once again, no sugar is used.

INGREDIENTS:

1 medium head red cabbage
2 medium apples
oil for cooking
1 cup water
3 tablespoons apple cider vinegar
3 tablespoons honey
salt and pepper to taste

1. Shred cabbage, discarding core.
2. Peel, core, and chop apples.
3. Heat wok over medium heat.
4. Necklace with oil.
5. Add cabbage and all remaining ingredients except salt and pepper.
6. Mix well. Cook over lower heat and cook slowly, until cabbage is tender.
7. Check seasoning. Add salt and pepper to taste. Add more vinegar if desired.
8. Serve.

Mr. Lee's Snow Peas in Oyster Sauce

Snow peas are Chinese peas that are enjoyed pod and all. They are a tender Oriental delicacy. Be sure to try them next time they're in season, or try the frozen. Oyster sauce is a super thing to flavor with and a bottle costs about a dollar. The most readily available is put out by Dynasty and is generally found at Chinese vegetable stands or, if you are lucky, in your grocery store near the soy sauce.

Again, this recipe is from the very creative gourmets, Mr. and Mrs. Lee.

INGREDIENTS:

¼ pound snow peas
oil for cooking
1–2 tablespoons oyster sauce
1 teaspoon water
salt and pepper to taste

1. Wash the pea pods carefully and remove the hard little stems at either end.
2. Heat wok and necklace with oil.
3. Add pods and toss.
4. Sprinkle all over with oyster sauce and 1 teaspoon water, and gently keep stirring 3 to 5 minutes over medium heat.
5. Sit down and enjoy a true Oriental specialty!

The Martinied Eggplant

There is this sort of underground worldwide club that has no dues, no rules, no membership cards, and no scheduled meetings. As a matter of truth, all the members have only one thing in common and one recognizable password. It's simply: ". . . and I'll take a martini, please." It doesn't matter if it's straight up or on the rocks, with a twist or with an olive. A martini is a martini and one martini lover an immediate cohort with another!

I have a favorite martini lover myself. His name is Jerry Laks. He and his wife, Cathy, have had an enormous influence on my life. We met by chance in the backwoods of the eastern shore of Maryland, where they lived in a beautifully converted chicken house, selling handcrafted candles by day and sipping martinis by twilight. I was in the incredibly painful throes of youth when we met and around the martinis floated endless hours of philosophical, literary, and personal discussion. They were a light in the darkness, as they still are for me today. The original manuscript of this book was written in their home, many of the recipes tested in their kitchen and shared by all of us. Our times together are favorite moments of my life and I thank them for letting me become part of their family. This recipe was created for Jerry, my mellow mentor, and for martini lovers everywhere.

INGREDIENTS:

1 eggplant
1 green pepper
1 onion
oil for cooking
1 tablespoon sesame seeds
1 jigger of gin
salt and pepper to taste
½ teaspoon white vermouth

1. Wash eggplant and cut into 1-inch cubes. Set aside.
2. Wash green pepper and cut into 1-inch strips. Set aside.
3. Peel onion and slice. Set aside.
4. Heat wok.
5. Necklace with oil.
6. Add sesame seeds and onion. Toss for 3 minutes.
7. Add green pepper. Toss for 3 minutes.
8. Add eggplant, toss, and cover. Stir fry for 5 minutes over medium heat.
9. Add gin, raise heat, and stir constantly. Add salt and pepper to taste. Add vermouth.
10. When all vegetables are very tender, enjoy your martini!

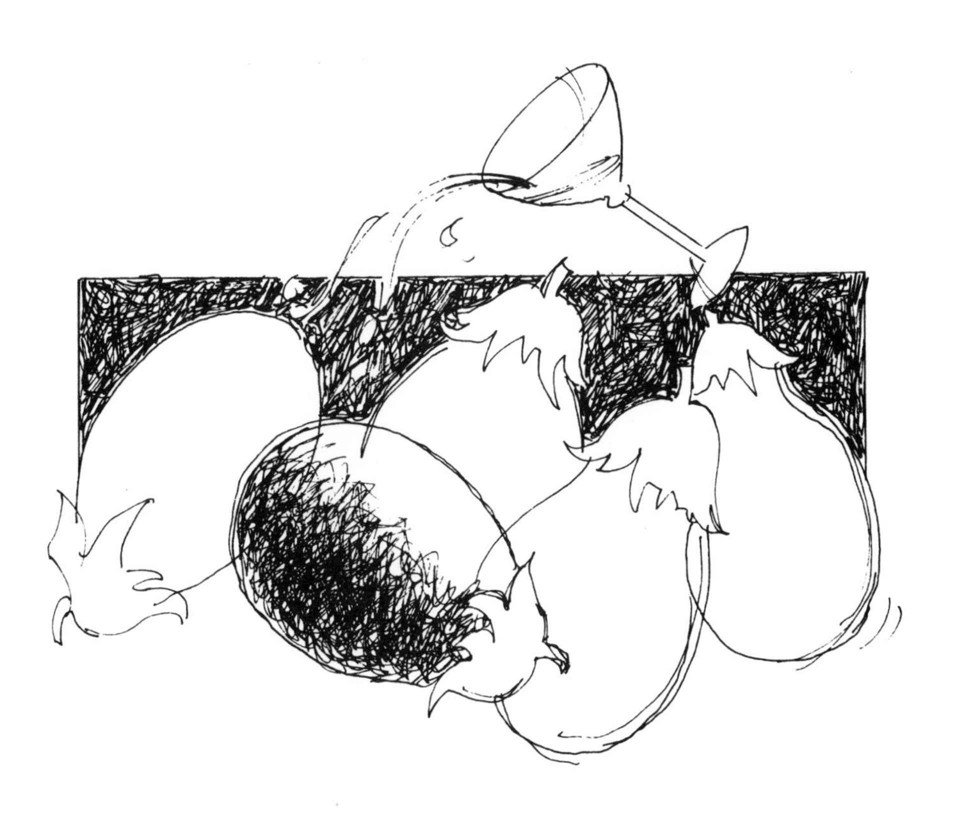

String Beans and Potatoes

Homey and warm . . . a toasty combination I've been eating all my life. It tastes even better now that it's wokked!

INGREDIENTS:

1 clove fresh garlic
1 pound string beans
3 medium potatoes
oil for cooking
1 tablespoon sesame seeds
2 uncooked bacon slices in 1-inch pieces
¼ cup boiling water
2 tablespoons butter
salt and pepper to taste

1. Mince garlic. Set aside.
2. Wash string beans with cool water, clip strings, and snap in half. Set aside.
3. Scrub potatoes (remember not to peel) and cut into quarters. Set aside.
4. Heat wok.
5. Necklace with oil.
6. Add seeds and garlic, and stir fry till golden.
7. Add beans, and toss to coat with oil. Add bacon pieces.
8. Add potatoes and toss to coat with oil.
9. Add boiling water.
10. Add butter, salt, and pepper. Cover and stir occasionally.
11. Cook until potatoes are tender and serve.

Hot Spinach and Mushrooms

The combination of spinach and mushrooms is a widespread favorite as a cold salad. Now try it hot for a tasty change.

INGREDIENTS:

1 pound fresh spinach
½ pound fresh mushrooms
1 clove garlic
oil for cooking
1 tablespoon sesame seeds
salt and pepper to taste
2 tablespoons butter

1. Wash spinach well (it's sandy), clip stalky stems, and set aside.
2. Wash mushrooms. Trim bottom of stalk and make vertical slices and set aside.
3. Mince garlic. Set aside.
4. Heat wok.
5. Necklace with oil.
6. Add seeds and garlic, and stir fry till golden.
7. Add mushrooms, toss and stir for 3 minutes.
8. Add spinach, toss, and cover.
9. As spinach cooks down, sprinkle with salt and pepper.
10. Dot with butter and allow to melt.
11. Serve when hot and tender.

Italian Wax Beans and Potatoes in Tomato Sauce

What can I say? Tomato sauce and Parmesan cheese, my favorites, team up in this one to make it the zestiest vegetable combination imaginable.

INGREDIENTS:

1 pound wax beans*
3 medium potatoes
1 clove garlic
oil for cooking
1 tablespoon sesame seeds
2 small cans of tomato sauce
pinch of sugar
dash of wine
salt and pepper to taste
¼ cup grated Parmesan cheese (plus extra for topping)

1. Wash beans, clip ends, and set aside.
2. Wash potatoes, cube, and set aside.
3. Mince garlic. Set aside.
4. Heat wok.
5. Necklace with oil.
6. Add garlic and seeds, and stir fry until golden.
7. Add tomato sauce and stir.
8. Add sugar and wine, stir, and simmer over low heat 10 minutes covered.
9. Add beans, cover, and simmer 5 minutes.
10. Add potatoes, salt and pepper, and simmer until tender.
11. Add Parmesan cheese, stir well, and simmer 2 to 3 minutes.
12. Serve with additional Parmesan cheese—it's great on top.

*String beans can easily be substituted.

Zucchini Fritters

These are really unusual and definite crowd pleasers. Who ever said vegetables had to be boring?

INGREDIENTS:

1 egg, beaten
1 large zucchini, grated
¼–½ cup corn flake crumbs
2 tablespoons Parmesan cheese, grated
1 tablespoon fresh chopped parsley
3 cups oil*
tamari

1. Mix all ingredients except oil in medium-size bowl. Refrigerate ½ hour.
2. Heat 3 cups oil in wok.
3. Drop batter by the tablespoon into hot oil a *few* at a time (too many at once will lower the temperature).
4. Remove, blot with paper towel, and serve at once.
5. Dip in tamari sauce.

*After oil cools down, strain and pour into storage container for reuse.

Golden Country Corn Fritters*

INGREDIENTS:

1⅓ cup sifted flour
1½ teaspoons baking powder
1 teaspoon salt
1 17-ounce can cream-style corn
1 egg, slightly beaten
2 scallions minced
¼ cup chopped fresh parsley
3 cups corn oil**

1. Sift flour with baking powder and salt.
2. Mix corn and egg and add rest of ingredients except oil.
3. Heat oil in wok over medium heat (to about 370° F.).
4. Drop batter by the tablespoon into hot oil. Don't put too many in at once.
5. Remove when golden on all sides. Drain on paper towels. Serve hot.

*Makes 32 fritters.
**When oil cools down, strain and pour into storage container for reuse.

Magic Mushrooms

INGREDIENTS:

4 large, firm mushrooms
½ cup milk
¾ cup flour
1 egg
salt to taste
2 cups oil for cooking

1. Wash and slice mushrooms into vertical slices.
2. Make a smooth batter out of milk, flour, egg, and salt.
3. Heat 2 cups oil in wok.
4. Dip slices in batter and fry on both sides until light brown. Serve hot.

Wok Corn

That's right—popcorn in a wok! The shape of the wok is perfect here again. Paul, a friend of the family, suggested I try it and, sure enough, it's a great popcorn popper.

Follow the directions of the popcorn you're using, but forget the popper and do it right in your wok!

Vegetables as a Main Dish

By now, I'm guessing, the idea of vegetables has gotten too big to be contained on the side of that plate any longer!

So here they are . . . vegetable dishes that worked right into the main courses!!!

Zucchini and Pasta

(The dish that made Grandma and Annette famous)

This has to be the easiest, most economical dish there is. It was born in a farm kitchen in Stockton, Maryland, and later was said to resemble one of my Grandma's dishes that had been forgotten. This recipe has been picked up by friends I've made all over the country, and so have countless variations. Here's how it began—you take it from there.

INGREDIENTS:

- 2–3 yellow squash or zucchini or any combination of the two
- 2 scallions
- ¼ pound more or less of mushrooms
- ½ pound pasta (long thin spaghetti works great . . . spinach noodles are an interesting change)
- oil for cooking
- 1 clove fresh garlic, minced
- 2 tablespoons sesame seeds
- salt and pepper to taste
- pinch of thyme
- ½ cup Parmesan cheese, grated (plus extra for topping)
- ¼ cup butter (you can substitute margarine, but of course—it isn't the same!)

1. Wash the zucchini very well (they're sandy). Also wash the scallions and the mushrooms.
2. Slice the zucchini thinly and set aside.
3. Chop the scallions. Set aside.
4. Slice the mushrooms. Set aside.
5. Start water boiling for pasta, cook as directed with salt.
6. Heat wok.
7. Necklace with oil. Add garlic.
8. Add sesame seeds and scallions. Stir fry 2 minutes.

9. Add the squash a few slices at a time and stir to cover all sides with oil.
10. As the squash begins to fry golden, add the mushrooms. Keep stirring.
11. Season with salt and pepper and a pinch of thyme.
12. Add oil only if you need it to keep everything from sticking.
13. Cook only till veggies are crisp and tender.
14. When pasta is done, drain and immediately add cheese and butter and toss.
15. To serve, place a portion of pasta on each plate and ladle veggies on top. Of course, sprinkle additional Parmesan.

That's it! It costs about a dollar a person at the most, and it's so-o-o good!

Variations can begin with adding green pepper and/or tomato and go anywhere. In this one, imagination is everything.

Squash and Potatoes Italiano

This is another dish whose origin goes back far with me. I first tried making it in college when, in the face of dormitory food, I got myself a hot plate. My roommate, Mary, was the first of many to wrinkle her nose at the sound of it and then proceed to wolf it down after a timid taste. Years after college, it became the dish I always brought to those "everybody bring something" feasts that happen occasionally. It was the perfect choice to bring a lot of, since it is inexpensive, and easy to make and transport. It also happens to be absolutely delicious. Besides, no one else *ever* brought it and whether it was a yoga ashram or a Tupperware party, it was a sure hit!

It's actually amazingly convenient to make for a lot of people. One night I remember making it in the country for dinner for myself. Just as I was cutting up the squash, a car pulled up with a few friends. We all decided we were starving, so I just kept cutting up more squash. Not five minutes later, I heard the rumble of tires on the gravel again. Sure enough, a little green van pulled up filled with fine, familiar faces who, of course, were also starved. It was the perfect dish to have been making. I just cut up more of everything, filled the wok to capacity, and within about a half hour twelve people sat down to dinner!

INGREDIENTS:

1 clove garlic
1 small onion
4–5 zucchini or yellow squash
3–4 potatoes
oil for cooking
1 tablespoon sesame seeds
2 small cans tomato sauce
pinch of sugar
dash of wine
pinch of oregano
salt and pepper to taste
½ cup Parmesan cheese, grated

1. Mince garlic and set aside.
2. Peel and chop onion and set aside.
3. Wash squash (or zucchini), cut into chunks and set aside.
4. Wash potatoes well and cut into 1-inch cubes. Set aside.
5. Heat wok.
6. Necklace with oil.
7. Add garlic and sesame seeds and onion; stir fry until golden.
8. Add tomato sauce, sugar, and wine; simmer 5 minutes.
9. Add zucchini (or squash) and let cook 5 minutes.
10. Add potatoes, oregano, salt and pepper; stir and cover.
11. When potatoes are tender, it's ready.
12. Sprinkle heavily with Parmesan cheese and serve.
13. Again additional parmesan is yummy.

Hope you have leftovers, because the next day it's just as good or better heated up!

Pepper Pie

Picture if you will . . . eleven o'clock on a Friday night . . . a tired cheerleader coming home . . . an incredible mother still up to feed her. Too tired and wound up to eat a heavy dinner, the solution is obvious to them both—Pepper Pie!

Well, the cheerleader is gone for sure, but the mother is still incredible, and the Pepper Pie goes on forever.

INGREDIENTS:

1 small to medium green pepper
5 eggs
2 tablespoons milk
salt and pepper to taste
oil for cooking
1 tablespoon sesame seeds

1. Cut up green pepper into about 1-inch pieces.
2. Beat eggs with milk and salt and pepper.
3. Heat wok.
4. Necklace with oil.
5. Add sesame seeds and pepper pieces. Cover.
6. Cook until pepper is really tender.
7. Add egg mixture and stir.
8. Cook until desired consistency and serve.

The Italian Mother's Chicken Soup*

(or Squash with Poached Egg)

Okay, now I know this one sounds a little far out there, but hold on. You've come this far with me—come just a little bit farther and try an old Italian remedy for a tired stomach.

When I said your wok was versatile, I really meant it. Maybe no Italian mama ever used a wok, but this Italian baby found it turns out the best Squash with Poached Egg ever! So go ahead and try it when someone you care about needs light nourishment. It's gentle on the innards, its most important ingredient being love.

INGREDIENTS:

2 small zucchini or yellow squash
1 tablespoon fresh parsley
½ cup water
1 tablespoon oil
salt and pepper to taste
1 egg

1. Wash zucchini and cut into thin slices. Set aside.
2. Wash parsley and mince. Set aside.
3. Add water to wok. Turn on high heat. Add oil.
4. Add parsley and salt and pepper. Boil for 3 minutes.
5. Add zucchini, making sure water just covers it.
6. Cover and boil 10 to 15 minutes till tender.
7. Break egg on top, cover, and let cook 3 minutes.
8. Serve tenderly with broth.

*Serves 1.

German Noodles and Cabbage à la Aunt Jean*

I first came to New York as a hopeful, budding starlet . . . and soon became a typical starving actress. Between auditions and classes and "go-see's," a hot meal was a thing I only faintly remembered. Well, they say every artist needs a guardian and they're probably right. Mine was Aunt Jean. Aunt Jean and Uncle John filled those hard days with encouragement, understanding, and good food. It was during this period that I first tasted Noodles and Cabbage. It became an inside joke between us—they never had to ask anymore what I'd like for dinner. They knew.

To this day, Noodles and Cabbage holds as much for me in memories as it does in taste. Uncle John grated the cabbage, Aunt Jean put it all together, and Annette just ate! We'd like to share it with you now.

INGREDIENTS:

4 pounds cabbage
½ teaspoon salt and salt to taste
4 slices bacon
oil for cooking
½ pound sweet butter
pepper to taste
1 pound wide egg noodles

1. Grate cabbage into shreds, add ½ teaspoon salt, and mix well. Set aside for at least ½ hour or overnight stored in refrigerator.
2. Dice bacon.
3. Heat wok.
4. Necklace with oil.
5. Add bacon and brown.

*Serves 6—with leftovers.

6. When bacon is browned, add butter.
7. Squeeze cabbage to remove excess water.
8. Add cabbage to wok, mixing with butter and bacon.
9. Add salt and pepper to taste.
10. Simmer covered, 1 hour until tender, stirring occasionally.
11. Cook noodles as directed. Drain. Then combine with cabbage.
12. Remove entire wok and dok from heat and set aside. Aunt Jean says, "The longer it sits, the better it is!"
13. Heat over low flame and enjoy.

Vegetarian Delight

Cities aren't so easy to live in these days—just ask anyone who lives in the country and they'll be glad to tell you all about it. Somehow, however, many of us see enough sparkling in the cement to continue with them. If you *do* live in a city, one thing becomes an absolute necessity to get through the daily rigors—good health . . . just plain feeling *good*. City health stores flourish as more and more people become aware of the true necessity to feed their bodies well, and this year parks are blooming with as many people as flowers.

A lot of those people are roller skating and running . . . not away from anything this time, but into a whole new healthy world of body awareness. Exercise can help change not only your body shape, but your mental state as well. As one who greeted the high school 600-yard run-walk as something of a nightmare, it was tough getting out there that first time! But once you're out, you'll find it's easy. Exercise can be a real joy and has helped me immeasurably in the past few years. Many people find it so fantastic, it becomes a main force in their life-style.

My friend Jonathan Elliott is one of them. I had been running for a few years but hadn't attempted roller skating since Girl Scouts. Well, under his gentle direction I got back on skates and was soon flying around Central Park and loving it! The only thing that gets me off skates these days is hunger. After a fun day in the park, I'm starving and head home for a yummy, high-energy dinner. For me, it's the start of a perfect evening. Next is one of my favorites. It's light, low in calories, and filled with energy . . . Vegetarian Delight!

Consider this recipe merely a match with which to light your own creativity. Be sure to take advantage of the pick of the season's vegetables in your area. Before embarking on the preparation, check out what's in your own refrigerator that can be added. With cheese on top and brown rice underneath, it's a complete and nutritious dinner.

INGREDIENTS:

1 medium onion or 2 scallions
1 squash
¼ pound mushrooms
1 small head broccoli
¼ pound snow peas
1 tomato
oil for cooking
salt and pepper to taste
tamari to taste (remember, it's salty!)
3 slices Muenster cheese
hot cooked brown rice

1. Slice up onion. Set aside.
2. Wash and slice squash. Set aside.
3. Wash and slice mushrooms. Set aside.
4. Break broccoli into flowerets and wash. Set aside.
5. Clip stems on snow peas and wash. Set aside.
6. Rinse and chop up tomato. Set aside.
7. Heat wok.
8. Necklace with oil.
9. Add onions and stir fry 1 minute.
10. Add squash a few slices at a time, toss and stir fry till beginning to turn brown.
11. Add broccoli and toss to cover with oil.
12. Add snow peas, tomato, and mushrooms. Stir to mix well.
13. Season with salt and pepper and tamari. Add more oil if necessary and continue cooking.
14. As vegetables get tender, cut cheese into strips and lay them on top. Sprinkle sides of wok with cold water and cover to create steam.
15. When cheese is melted, serve immediately over rice.

Eggs and Omelets

One of the nicest surprises in Wokcookery happens at breakfast. Forget the idea of having to buy special omelet pans to make great eggs. You already own one! Your wok turns out fluffy, yummy omelets, and it's *so* easy!

When preparing wokked eggs, just remember to go lightly on the oil. Merely *drizzle* that necklace of oil and then tilt wok from side to side to cover the surface.

Always be aware that you're cooking over high heat, so stir constantly, and when eggs begin to set, flip over with your flat lifter, cook a second or two longer, and lift out.

Breakfasts are beginnings, so enjoy, my friends, enjoy. (All breakfast recipes are written to serve two, because it's more fun than eating alone!)

Sesame Scrambled Eggs

INGREDIENTS:

1 scallion
4 eggs, beaten
2 tablespoons milk
oil for cooking
2 tablespoons sesame seeds
salt and pepper to taste

1. Chop scallion into fine pieces. Set aside.
2. Beat eggs and milk with fork or wire whisk. Set aside.
3. Heat wok over medium-high flame.
4. Drizzle a necklace of oil around top.
5. Immediately add seeds and onion, stirring constantly with a wooden spoon or chopsticks until seeds start to pop and onion is golden.
6. Pour in eggs and season with salt and pepper.
7. Continue stirring until eggs are the consistency you like.
8. Lift out and serve.

Brian's Favorite—Eggs with Zucchini and Muenster Cheese

If anyone knows Annette Annechild's Wokcookery, it's Brian Quill. He has shared and helped create more feasts with me than anyone I know. He also allows my eccentricities to flourish, understanding it all as art. He has never once shied away from 3 A.M. wokked carrot cake or dinners of breakfast omelets. He's a true friend.

This omelet is our collaboration and our favorite Sunday brunch. We hope you enjoy it as we do.

INGREDIENTS:

1 scallion
1 small zucchini
4 eggs
2 tablespoons milk
salt and pepper to taste
¼ teaspoon basil
pinch of thyme
oil for cooking
1 tablespoon sesame seeds
2 slices Muenster cheese, cut into thick strips

1. Chop scallion into small pieces. Set aside.
2. Slice zucchini. Set aside.
3. Beat eggs with milk, salt and pepper, basil, and thyme.
4. Heat wok over high heat.
5. Necklace with oil.
6. Add zucchini. Stir fry 3 to 5 minutes or until tender.
7. Add seeds and onion and stir fry 3 to 5 minutes.
8. Add egg mixture. Stir.
9. When almost to desired consistency, flip over. Lay strips of cheese across top. Sprinkle around sides of wok with cold water, and cover. This will create steam and melt cheese quickly.
10. When cheese is melted, serve.

The Creamy, Cheesy, Nutty Omelet

Blame it on my years in New York City, but whenever I hear cream cheese I think of "Chock full o' nuts" and date nut bread. What could be better than your own creamy cheese omelet and warm date nut bread to start a day? Not much in my experience—not much at all.

INGREDIENTS:

4–6 walnuts
5 eggs
2 tablespoons milk
salt and pepper to taste
oil for cooking
2 tablespoons cream cheese

1. Chop nuts into small pieces and set aside.
2. Beat eggs with milk and salt and pepper, using a fork or wire whisk.
3. Heat wok.
4. Necklace lightly with oil.
5. Add eggs and stir.
6. As eggs begin to set, add cream cheese in little bits and sprinkle in nuts. Keep stirring.
7. When eggs are the consistency you like, lift out and serve.

Eggplant Eric

Eggplant is really a sensational vegetable because there is so much you can *do* with it. Eggplant and eggs, no matter how strange it may sound to you, is a super combination.

We discovered it one morning in Wattsville, Virginia, during the writing of this book. Eric is Cathy and Jerry's nephew and I have him to thank for interspersing music with the long hours of recipe writing. He made the room come alive with beautiful melodies, and I don't think I ever enjoyed singing more.

Eggplant Eric came into existence on a morning of writing and music, and after one taste we knew it was a must for this book.

INGREDIENTS:

- 1 small onion
- 5 eggs
- 2 tablespoons milk
- salt and pepper to taste
- oil for cooking
- 1 tablespoon sesame seeds
- 1 teaspoon poppy seeds
- ½ cup small sliced pieces of eggplant
- 2 slices Muenster cheese

1. Slice onion into small pieces. Set aside.
2. Beat eggs with milk, using fork or wire whisk, and season with salt and pepper.
3. Heat wok.
4. Necklace with oil.
5. Add onion and seeds and stir fry.
6. Add eggplant and stir fry until golden.
7. Add eggs and stir.
8. As eggs reach desired consistency, flip and place cheese in strips across top.
9. Sprinkle with cold water and cover tightly to create steam.
10. When cheese is melted, serve.

Note: When you make the Martinied Eggplant in the Veggies section, just save a little eggplant out for the next day's breakfast.

Golden Green

Some people think of late sleepers as rather lazy people. Being super into mornings, I must admit to once believing that. I hadn't realized that many late sleepers are just night people who couldn't let go of even *one* of their magical hours. It's when the music gets written or the song gets sung.

For them, brunch is a most important meal, since it comes after too many hours of not eating and is counted on to hold them until evening. With that in mind, nothing could be better than an omelet. My way to make them is full of protein and vitamins, yet light enough to put on that empty stomach.

So if you've got a family or a friend into night hours and late sleeping—or maybe just on a lazy Sunday morning—be sure to try one of these.

If a recipe can be dedicated, this one's for Sahm, an artist who fed my head with music and inspired me to create Golden Green . . . an omelet as healthful and delicious as it is beautiful.

INGREDIENTS:

5 eggs
2 tablespoons milk
salt and pepper to taste
oil for cooking
¾ cup cooked, cut-up spinach, well drained*
1 tablespoon sesame seeds
¼ cup shredded cheddar cheese
parsley flakes (optional)
sour cream (optional)
toast (optional)

1. Beat eggs and milk with fork or wire whisk and season with salt and pepper. Set aside.
2. Heat wok.
3. Necklace with oil.
4. Add spinach and seeds and stir fry 3 minutes.
5. Add eggs and stir.

6. When eggs are partially set, flip over and sprinkle with cheese.
7. Sprinkle sides of wok with cold water and cover to create steam. When cheese is melted, lift out.
8. Sprinkle with parsley flakes and serve with sour cream and toast.

*Usually, this is an ideal way to use up leftover spinach. However, if you need to cook up some fresh, it's easy. Wash well (it's sandy) and break off thick stems. Place ¼ cup water in your wok with 1 teaspoon salt and 1 teaspoon pepper and turn on high heat. When boiling, add spinach, toss, and cover. Spinach will cook down to a fraction of its original size. When tender, turn off heat and cool. Drain and cut up.

Soups*

Ah . . . *now* your wok will prove its versatility in still *another* area. What a great soup pot it is!

The most delicious soups I've ever tasted were made in a wok. The seasonings built up in the patina of your wok will enhance the flavor of every soup you make in it. It also serves as an interesting tureen that can be brought right to the table.

I do feel it's ideal, however, to have a separate wok for soups. The long boiling and simmering process that soups entail can eventually break down the patina built up from stir frying. Buying a separate wok need not mean buying a whole set. You can use the same cover and dok and utensils. A simple 14 to 16 inch wok is very inexpensive and will serve you well. If you *do* begin using two woks, also use the soup wok for your steaming and poaching—keeping the other strictly for stir frying and omelet making.

*Yields for all the soup recipes are a wokful!

Vegetable Stock

Now here's a way to use up all those seeds and stems and leftover vegetable pieces. Make a healthy stock with them! Keep a plastic bag in your refrigerator and save all onion skins and wilted lettuce leaves and any and all leftover vegetable parts. When you have a full bag you've a good start on a really great soup stock. Stock freezes very well, so use what you need and put the rest up for later.

INGREDIENTS:

3 medium carrots
2 potatoes
1 onion
2 tomatoes
all saved leftovers
cold water
½ cup parsley, chopped
1 teaspoon thyme
1 bay leaf
salt and pepper to taste

1. Wash the vegetables and place in wok with leftovers.
2. Fill with cold water till wok is ¾ full.
3. Bring to boiling. Reduce heat and simmer covered.
4. After about an hour, add the parsley, thyme, and bay leaf. Simmer covered for another ½ hour or so.
5. Strain thru sieve. Season with salt and pepper.
6. Serve as is or use as a base for any other soup in place of water. It's also ideal for making rice, substituting it for water.

Grandma's Lentil Soup

When I was very little, I used to spend a lot of afternoons with my grandma. She was absolutely renowned as the chef of the family and was constantly cooking up something. I watched her cook for years and then, as I got older, promptly dismissed what I'd seen. Years later Grandma died and everyone sadly realized her incredible unwritten recipes were lost forever.

Well, in the late sixties "health food" really became the "in" thing. Being very much a part of the growing movement, I got interested. One day I was in a health food store and saw lentils. Suddenly, in a flash, I remembered! I remembered watching Grandma with those tiny little beans and, what's more, I remembered what she did with them.

Grandma's cooking was health food without ever calling it that. Her presence is felt throughout this book and this is her very own lentil soup.

INGREDIENTS:

1 cup lentils
6 cups water or stock
1 teaspoon salt
1 stalk celery
3 carrots
2 onions
2 tablespoons oil
2 tablespoons sesame seeds

1. Rinse lentils with cold water.
2. Place 6 cups stock or water, 1 teaspoon salt, and lentils in wok and heat.
3. Bring just to boiling, lower heat, cover, and simmer ½ hour.
4. Meanwhile, wash and slice veggies.
5. Heat in separate skillet (or that other wok if you've got it) 2 tablespoons oil.

6. Add celery, seeds, carrots, and onion. Stir fry 5 to 7 minutes.
7. Add to wok.
8. Simmer 15 minutes and serve.

With a loaf of good bread and perhaps a salad, you've got it made!

My Chicken Vegetable Soup

Everybody's got their own chicken soup recipe. Here's mine.

INGREDIENTS:

- chicken parts (back, necks, and whatever)
- cold water
- 2 bay leaves
- pinch of basil
- 2 tablespoons chopped fresh parsley
- 4–5 scallions
- a handful of mushrooms
- ½ pound snow peas
- 5 carrots
- 2 stalks celery
- 1 tomato
- pinches of thyme, garlic salt, oregano, salt and pepper
- 1 small can tomato sauce
- pastina egg noodles or rice or elbow macaroni
- parmesan cheese, grated

1. Wash chicken, then place in wok and fill ¾ full with cold water.
2. Add bay leaves, basil, and parsley.
3. Cover, bring to boil, and then let simmer.
4. Meanwhile, wash and cut veggies. Set aside.
5. After an hour or so, when chicken is very tender, remove from wok. Let cool and remove all meat from bones. Add to wok.
6. Add rest of seasonings.
7. Add veggies and tomato sauce and salt and pepper to taste. Simmer as long as possible.
8. Add rice or pasta in last minutes of cooking.
9. Add amount you desire, but remember they get bigger and absorb water. The soup is done when the pasta is.
10. Serve piping hot, topped with lots of additional Parmesan cheese.

Miso Soup

Miso is one of the most incredible foods ever invented by man. Miso has a unique flavor that makes a great base for soups and also provides a healthful balance of essential oils, minerals, natural sugars, proteins, and vitamins.

It is a dark brown paste that is usually sold in plastic packets in a health food store. It's very different and *very* worth trying.

One tip on miso soup making: never let it boil once you add the miso paste. It destroys some of the most nutritionally valuable ingredients.

INGREDIENTS:

2 carrots
1 onion or 1–2 scallions
¼ head of cabbage
sesame oil for cooking
5 cups water
¼ teaspoon salt
4 tablespoons miso paste

1. Wash carrots and onion and thinly slice.
2. Wash cabbage and cut into strips.
3. Heat wok.
4. Necklace with oil.
5. Add onions, cabbage, and carrots. Stir fry for 10 minutes.
6. Add ½ cup water and bring veggies to boil.
7. Lower flame, cover, and simmer 15 minutes.
8. Add remaining water and salt and simmer 15 minutes.
9. Remove 1 ladle of stock and add miso paste to it. Stir till dissolved.
10. Add to wok. Stir. Cover and turn flame off.
11. Let set for 5 minutes, then serve.

Note: For variety, add mushrooms or squash (in step 5).

French Onion Soup*

INGREDIENTS:

oil for cooking
4 cups onion, thinly sliced
5 cups stock
1 teaspoon salt
4 french bread slices
2 tablespoons Parmesan cheese, grated
8 slices mozzarella cheese

1. Heat wok.
2. Necklace with oil.
3. Add onions and stir fry till golden—about 6 to 8 minutes.
4. Add stock and salt. Lower heat and simmer, covered, for 30 minutes.
5. Brown bread on both sides under broiler.
6. Pour soup into ovenproof bowls and float 1 slice bread in each.
7. Sprinkle with Parmesan and lay 2 slices of mozzarella cheese on top of each.
8. Put under broiler until cheese is golden and bubbly.

*Serves 4.

Rosebud's Cream of Tomato and Rice Soup

Somewhere in the hills of Maryland's eastern shore roams the bulldog of your dreams. Rosebud captured the hearts of the clan at the Candle Factory in Wattsville, Virginia and one day captured the just-wokked tomato rice soup! It was gone to the last lick and we consider *that* Rosebud's recommendation!

INGREDIENTS:

1 clove garlic
2 carrots
2 scallions
6 mushrooms
oil for cooking
1 teaspoon sesame seeds
2 tablespoons whole wheat flour
3 cups stock or water
7 fresh tomatoes, cut up, or canned equivalent
1 teaspoon salt
4 white peppercorns
1 tablespoon fresh chopped parsley
1 teaspoon sugar
1 teaspoon oregano
1 teaspoon basil
1 bay leaf
1 pint half-and-half
1 cup cooked rice
2 tablespoons butter

1. Mince garlic. Set aside.
2. Wash and slice carrots, scallions, and mushrooms. Set aside.
3. Heat wok.
4. Necklace with oil.
5. Stir fry garlic.
6. Add carrots, scallions, mushrooms, and sesame seeds till seeds and onions are golden. Add flour and mix.

7. Add stock, tomatoes, salt, peppercorns, parsley, sugar, and herbs.
8. Simmer 1 hour.
9. Puree in blender. Add half-and-half, rice, and butter.
10. Reheat slowly without boiling.
11. Serve.

SAUCES

An excellent sauce turns the simplest fare into a specialty. There is no need to be intimidated by any of these sauce recipes—they only *taste* difficult to make. In reality, they are dependable, easy recipes that, atop your wokked vegetables or seafood, will make you feel like an international chef. If you own a wire whisk, now's the time to pull it out; a wooden spoon will work, but a wire whisk is really the best for sauces.

Basic White Sauce

This is really one to master because you can add anything to it for variations and it does beautifully over vegetables, poultry, and fish as is.

INGREDIENTS:

¼ cup butter
¼ cup unsifted all-purpose flour
½ teaspoon salt
⅛ teaspoon white pepper
1 cup milk
1 cup chicken stock (canned is fine)

1. In wok, slowly heat butter over low heat until melted and golden, stirring constantly with wooden spoon.
2. Turn off heat and slowly add flour, salt, and pepper, stirring constantly until smooth.
3. Turn heat back on to medium. Add milk and stock a little at a time, stirring all the while.
4. Heat to consistency of heavy cream and serve.

Note: An excellent and easy variation is to add the juice of one lemon and/or ½ cup fresh chopped parsley.

Cheese Sauce

INGREDIENTS:

3 tablespoons butter
3 tablespoons flour
1½ cups milk
1 cup grated cheddar cheese
½ teaspoon salt
⅛ teaspoon paprika
⅛ teaspoon pepper
1 teaspoon caraway seeds.

1. In wok, over medium heat, melt the butter and stir in flour until blended.
2. Slowly pour in milk and keep stirring.
3. When sauce is smooth and hot, reduce the heat and stir in cheese.
4. Add seasonings and keep stirring till cheese is melted.
5. Serve over hot wokked veggies.

If you ever need a cheese sauce in a hurry, there is another option: Combine 1 can cheddar cheese soup with ½ can milk and beat with wire whisk over low heat until smooth and hot. Season with salt and pepper. Pour over hot veggies. It's not quite the same, but it's really good.

Note: Both white and cheese sauces are especially good over wokked cauliflower.

Almond Sauce

INGREDIENTS:

¾ cup butter
¾ cup slivered almonds, toasted
1 teaspoon poppy seeds

1. Melt butter in saucepan.
2. Add almonds and seeds.
3. Stir fry 1 minute.
4. Pour over fish or vegetables.

Dill Sauce

INGREDIENTS:

½ cup butter
1 tablespoon lemon juice
2 tablespoons fresh dill or 1 teaspoon dried dill

1. Melt butter in saucepan.
2. Add lemon juice and dill.
3. Stir constantly for 1 minute.
4. Pour over fish or vegetables.

Note: Both Almond and Dill sauces are especially good over fresh flounder or sole.

Ali's Easy Hollandaise

Russell Bennett and I worked really hard to make sure that this isn't another hollandaise that doesn't work. We searched it out and found that our friend, Ali, had the easiest recipe, and she made it in a blender. Here it is, failproof and fabulous.

INGREDIENTS:

1 stick sweet butter
4 egg yolks
2 tablespoons lemon juice
dash of white pepper
1 teaspoon Dijon mustard (optional)
½ teaspoon salt

1. Melt butter in small saucepan over low heat until hot and bubbly but not brown.
2. Put rest of ingredients in blender and blend 5 seconds on high speed.
3. Slowly add butter through hole in cover of blender while it is still going on high speed or remove cover and pour in slowly with motor on a low speed.
4. Serve!

Note: My favorites for hollandaise are stir-fried broccoli or fresh poached asparagus.

Russell Bennett's Sauce Alouette

INGREDIENTS:

1 8-ounce package Alouette cheese spiced with garlic and herbs
3 tablespoons white vermouth
½ cup half-and-half

1. Melt cheese with half-and-half in pot over low flame till it reaches a creamy consistency.
2. With a wire whisk, stir in white vermouth.
3. Blend till well heated and serve as a delicious topping for vegetables and seafood.

Note: This sauce is excellent over just about anything. My favorite for it is a vegetable combination.

Quick Tuna Sauce

INGREDIENTS:

1 can tuna packed in oil
1 tablespoon sesame seeds
2 cans tomato sauce (large)
dash of red wine
½ cup Parmesan cheese
½ teaspoon sugar
⅛ teaspoon oregano
salt and pepper

1. Heat wok.
2. Open tuna and drain oil into necklace around wok.
3. Add seeds and tuna and stir fry 3 minutes.
4. Pour in tomato sauce, add wine, and simmer.
5. Add half of the cheese to the sugar, oregano, and salt and pepper to taste.
6. Simmer as long as possible.
7. Serve over pasta, with rest of Parmesan cheese on the side.

Fire Island Clam Sauce

Not all that far from the bulging metropolis of Manhattan is the virtual paradise of Fire Island. In about an hour, you can leave everything in your city life behind and be walking barefoot on a beautiful beach in the Fire Island community of your choice. My choice is Kismet, one of the more quiet and laid-back ones. There is the beach during the day and at night The Inn and The Out for entertainment. The summer bartender at The Inn is Russ Meyer, who happens to be one of the finest clammers on the island. We'd wade in the water and find 'em and run home to cook 'em! Fire Island Clam Sauce soon became a specialty of the house.

INGREDIENTS:

3 cloves garlic
the day's catch of clams (2–3 dozen)
olive oil for cooking
2 large cans tomato sauce
¼ teaspoon oregano
½ teaspoon basil
salt and pepper to taste
1 teaspoon sugar
dash of red wine
grated Parmesan cheese

1. Mince the garlic. Set aside.
2. Scrub the clams and steam till open. Cut up clams if large. Set aside.
3. Heat wok.
4. Necklace with oil.
5. Stir fry garlic till it begins to turn golden.
6. Add clams and stir fry.
7. Add tomato sauce, seasonings, sugar, and wine.
8. Simmer covered ½ hour.
9. Serve over pasta and top with Parmesan cheese.

My Mama's Truly Italian Spaghetti Sauce

Here it is, the queen of all the sauces! The recipe has been in my family for years and is guaranteed authentic and perfect for your wok!

INGREDIENTS:

1 large can (2-pounds, 3-ounces) Italian peeled plum tomatoes (with basil if possible)
1 clove garlic
olive oil for cooking
1 pound sausage or pork chops
1 small can tomato paste
grated Parmesan cheese
water
½ teaspoon salt or to taste
½ teaspoon sugar
¼ cup wine
1 basil leaf
¼ teaspoon oregano

1. Puree large can tomatoes in blender for one second or go through and remove stems and cores by hand. Set aside.
2. Mince garlic. Set aside.
3. Heat wok.
4. Necklace with olive oil.
5. Stir fry garlic till golden.
6. Pour in tomatoes and simmer.
7. Meanwhile, in skillet, brown sausage or pork chops. Then lift out and add to wok.
8. Remove excess fat from skillet, then place tomato paste and 1 can of water in it.
9. Add salt, sugar and wine, stir, and simmer 10 minutes.

10. Add to wok. Add basil and oregano, and simmer 2 hours.
11. Serve on pasta with grated Parmesan.

Note: To "stretch" sauce, Mom says, one 8-ounce can tomato sauce can be added.

Just Desserts: Sweetness and Light

In a country which probably consumes more refined sugar than any other on the planet, we desperately need a redefinition of desserts and treats. Having been a "sugar addict" and "junk food junkie" for years, I know just how hard it is to eliminate those treats that seem so special and so delicious. I will always want a great dessert after a great meal . . . but I have found there can be greatness with little or no sugar. Your wok can help you redefine your idea of dessert. No deprivation here—on the next pages you will find dazzling desserts that are sweetness and light. Fruits are used in new and exciting ways that practically eliminate the need for a sweetener. Honey is used whenever possible when a sweetener is needed because it is *much* better for you than refined white sugar. When a recipe does call for sugar, I've kept the amount to a minimum, and I recommend trying raw, brown, or date sugar as a substitute for the refined white. A sprinkling of wheat germ on any dessert will greatly increase its nutritional value. The fruit desserts are especially good for weight watchers. Even the cake recipes that follow are for light, more healthful cakes.

Wokcakery

That's right . . . Wokcakery! Enjoy your wok's most startling display of versatility yet. You can "bake" a cake in it—*steam* bake, that is. I could hardly get over it myself, but it works—it really does. The texture will be light and moist, the surface soft rather than crispy. The advantages of Wokcakery are many. It's energy saving, it's easy, and it's perfect in hot weather, when you don't want to heat up the house with the oven. Now you can even "bake" a cake when there's a turkey in your oven. You won't really believe it till you do it yourself, so have fun with one of these carefully tested recipes soon.

1. *Utensils*
   a. You will need a steam rack (a cake cooling rack is what I use).
   b. And a cake pan—a 6-cup round mold works well in a 14-inch to 16-inch wok. Also one 8-inch or 9-inch round layer cake pan is ideal.
2. *Procedure*
   a. Make batter according to the recipe.
   b. Pour into well-greased and floured cake pan.
   c. Place steam rack in wok.
   d. Pour in boiling water to just beneath rack.
   e. Place cake pan on rack.
   f. Cover tightly.
   g. Steam bake over medium heat.
3. *Tips for Wokcakery*
   a. All of the cake recipes in this book will work well in your wok. Other cake recipes will very often work as well. When trying other recipes, avoid or halve large recipes and eliminate using a lot of nuts, because they sometimes will create difficulty in the rising process.

b. Wok lids generally don't fit very tightly, so first, tent it!—use two sheets of aluminum foil, crossing one with the other over the top of the wok, and then cover with lid.

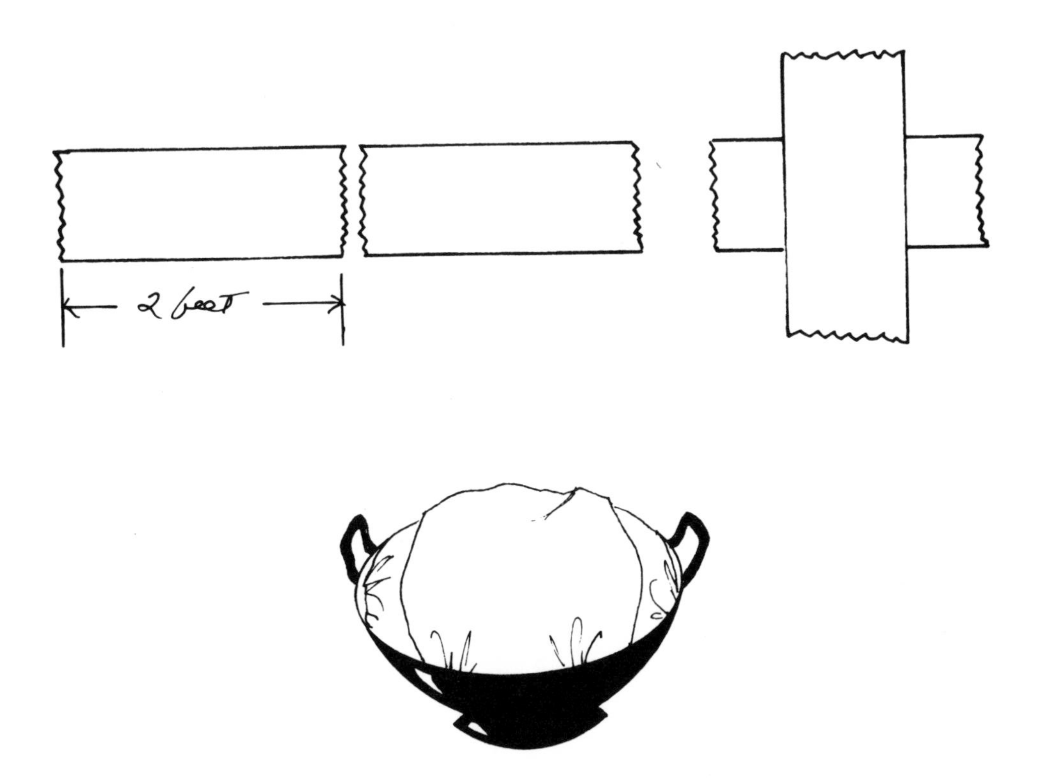

c. Boil water in a teakettle and add to wok under steam rack. Halfway through the baking time, check to be sure there is still water and add more if necessary.

d. Test your cake with a toothpick at the end of prescribed oven baking time. I have found steam baking takes a little more time.

e. Generally, use a medium heat to assure a gentle boil.

Feather-Light Sponge Cake Cardinal

INGREDIENTS:

6 eggs, separated
1 cup sugar
1 cup sifted flour
¼ cup cold water
1 teaspoon lemon juice
1 heaping teaspoon lemon rind
½ teaspoon cream of tartar
½ teaspoon salt
Cardinal Sauce (see recipe on opposite page)

1. With electric mixer, beat egg yolks till thick—about 5 minutes.
2. Beat sugar in gradually.
3. Beat in flour, alternating with cold water, lemon juice, and lemon rind. Set aside.
4. In large bowl, beat (using an electric mixer) egg whites with cream of tartar and salt till stiff.
5. Gradually and gently fold the egg yolk mixture into the stiff egg whites.
6. Pour into well-greased 10-inch tube pan mold. Cover loosely with a sheet of foil.
7. Place on rack over simmering water in covered wok for 45 minutes to 1 hour or until knife inserted comes out clean.
8. While cake is steaming, prepare Cardinal Sauce.
9. When cake is done, remove from wok and cool slightly. Place a cake rack over mold and invert. Cool cake on this rack.
10. Place cake on serving tray when cool. Top with Cardinal Sauce and serve.

CARDINAL SAUCE

INGREDIENTS:

- 3 tablespoons cornstarch
- 1¼ cup water
- 1 package (10-ounce) frozen raspberries, thawed
- 1 package (10-ounce) frozen strawberries, thawed

In saucepan, combine cornstarch with 1¼ cup water until smooth. Bring to boiling point. Boil, stirring until thickened and translucent, 5 to 8 minutes. Stir in berries. Let cool.

A Moist Little Chocolate Cake

INGREDIENTS:

- 1 cup flour
- 1 cup sugar
- ½ cup Hershey's cocoa (It matters!)
- 1 teaspoon baking powder
- ½ teaspoon salt
- 4 tablespoons butter
- 1 cup boiling water
- 1 teaspoon baking soda
- 1 egg
- 1 teaspoon vanilla

1. Sift flour, sugar, cocoa, baking powder, and salt into large bowl.
2. Mix thoroughly and push to sides of bowl.
3. In center of same bowl add butter and boiling water and then add baking soda to it. Let stand a few minutes till butter melts.
4. Then mix all together with wooden spoon.
5. Next add egg and vanilla. Mix well.
6. Pour into well-greased 9-inch round layer cake pan.
7. Place on steam rack in wok over simmering water. Cover.
8. Steam 35 minutes or until knife inserted comes out clean. Cool 10 minutes and remove from pan.
9. When cake is cooled, it can be sprinkled with powdered sugar and served with ice cream if desired.

Strawberry Steam Cakes*

INGREDIENTS:

2 cups fresh strawberries
2 cups flour
4 teaspoons baking powder
½ teaspoon salt
1 cup sugar
4 tablespoons butter
2 eggs, well beaten
1 cup milk

1. Slice well-washed strawberries. Set aside.
2. Mix flour, baking powder, salt and sugar.
3. Cut in the butter.
4. Add the eggs and strawberries and milk.
5. Pour into 6 well-greased custard cups.
6. Heat water beneath steam rack in wok.
7. Place cups on rack. Cover.
8. Steam 90 minutes. Remove from wok, cool 10 to 15 minutes, unmold, and enjoy. They're especially good with strawberry ice cream.

Note: A delicious variation can be made using cranberries or cherries. Pierce with needle before adding to batter.

---

*Makes 6 little cakes.

Gingerbread

INGREDIENTS:

¼ cup shortening
¼ cup sugar
¼ cup molasses
1 egg
¼ teaspoon ginger
¼ teaspoon cinnamon
1 cup flour
1 teaspoon soda
½ cup boiling water
whipped cream

1. Mix all ingredients together except the soda, water and cream.
2. Place soda on top of mixture and pour ½ cup boiling water over it, then mix all together.
3. Pour into greased and floured 6-cup mold.
4. Place on steam rack in wok over simmering water.
5. Cover and steam bake over medium heat 50 minutes or until inserted toothpick comes out clean. Cool 10 minutes and remove from pan.
6. Sprinkle with confectioner's sugar and serve with whipped cream.

Apple Sauce Cake

INGREDIENTS:

- 1¾ cups flour
- 1 teaspoon baking soda
- ½ teaspoon salt
- ½ teaspoon nutmeg
- ½ teaspoon cinnamon
- ¼ teaspoon cloves
- 1 cup brown sugar (firmly packed)
- ½ cup shortening
- 1 egg
- 1¼ cups apple sauce
- 1 cup raisins

1. Sift flour, baking soda, salt, and spices in small bowl. Set aside.
2. Beat brown sugar, shortening, and egg in 3-quart bowl until light and fluffy.
3. Mix dry ingredients alternately with apple sauce.
4. Stir in raisins.
5. Pour into 8-inch greased and floured pan.
6. Place on steam rack in wok over simmering water. Cover.
7. Steam bake over medium heat 50 minutes or until inserted toothpick comes out clean. Cool 10 minutes and remove from pan.

Note: You can sprinkle with confectioner's sugar and serve with whipped or ice cream.

Woodwind Carrot Cake

INGREDIENTS:

2 cups flour
2 cups sugar
1 teaspoon salt
2 teaspoon baking soda
2 teaspoons cinnamon
1½ cups oil
4 eggs, beaten
3 cups carrots, shredded
handful golden raisins

1. Sift dry ingredients together.
2. Add oil, eggs, carrots, and raisins.
3. Mix together with wooden spoon.
4. Pour batter into greased ring mold.
5. Place on steam rack in wok over simmering water. Cover.
6. Steam-bake 60 minutes or until knife inserted comes out clean.
7. Remove pan from wok. Cool 5 minutes and unmold.

Note: When cake is cooled, you can sprinkle with confectioner's sugar and serve with whipped cream or ice cream.

Honey Apples*

One cold and blustering winter evening, I was alone and working in my apartment, when from out of the blue . . . the munchies hit! And I mean *hit!* Now for me munchies mean something sweet, so I headed right for the kitchen. With disappointment edged slightly with panic, I discovered there was not one thing even remotely resembling dessert in my apartment. Now it was *cold* out, snowing, and it was late . . . *really* late. Pretty bleak picture, isn't it? Well, to make it worse, I had sworn off sugar for one week and I had one more day to make it through. The idea of searching through the city for something sweet *and* without sugar was too much to handle. I returned to the kitchen a little more desperate and a lot more willing to improvise.

"Well, there's an apple . . . (hm-m-m . . .) and there's honey . . . (getting better), and of course the wok is sitting right there . . . maybe a little flour, some cornstarch, an egg . . . (one last futile glance for an overlooked cookie). Sure, it's worth a try." Ten minutes later, there was one very pleased-with-herself lady happily munching away on honey apples.

These are great, quick, and no sugar! I guarantee they're *perfect* for the munchies!

INGREDIENTS:

3 tablespoons cornstarch
3 tablespoons flour
½ cup egg white
3 medium apples
1 cup oil for cooking
honey

---

*No sugar! Serves 4 to 6.

1. Mix cornstarch, flour, and egg white together with a wire whisk into a batter.
2. Slice the apples into 8 pieces each.
3. Heat oil in wok (about 375° F.).
4. Coat apple slices and drop into hot oil.
5. When golden on both sides, remove and drain on paper towels.
6. Arrange on platter and drizzle with honey.
7. Spear with toothpick.

Note: They are especially yummy sprinkled with fresh coconut and served next to a bowl of raisins.

Pear and Orange Fritters*

INGREDIENTS:

1 egg, separated
1 firm orange
1 ripe pear
½ lemon
1 tablespoon honey
½ cup sifted flour
pinch of salt
¼ cup milk
2 cups oil

1. Beat egg white and set aside when stiff.
2. Peel and wedge orange and slice pear. Put in a bowl.
3. Grate rind of ½ lemon over them and squeeze juice on top.
4. Drizzle with honey, stir to mix, and refrigerate.
5. Meanwhile sift flour and salt in bowl.
6. Add milk and egg yolk. Beat together.
7. Gently fold in egg white.
8. Heat 2 cups of oil in wok (to 375° F.).
9. Dip to coat pieces of fruit in batter.
10. Drop into oil.
11. Deep fry fruit till golden on both sides.
12. Drain on paper towels.

Note: Serve warm on toothpicks, drizzled with honey and sprinkled with coconut.

*Serves 4. Try all kinds of fresh fruity fritters: peaches, apples, and bananas work great, too. No white sugar here either!

Steam Baked Apples*

INGREDIENTS:

4 apples
¾ teaspoon salt
⅓ cup raisins or 6 chopped dates
⅓ cup apple juice
1 teaspoon coconut
½ teaspoon wheat germ
½ teaspoon cinnamon
¼ teaspoon nutmeg
optional: Grand Marnier Sauce (see recipe below)

1. Core apples and rub a small amount of salt on the inside. Place in baking dish.
2. Fill with raisins or dates.
3. Pour apple juice over apples.
4. Sprinkle with coconut and wheat germ, then cinnamon and nutmeg.
5. Place dish in rack over simmering water in wok.
6. Cover and steam 50 minutes, basting occasionally.
7. Serve with Grand Marnier Sauce (optional).

GRAND MARNIER SAUCE

INGREDIENTS:

1 pint sour cream
1 tablespoon honey
1–2 tablespoons Grand Marnier to taste

1. Blend ingredients together.
2. Pour over apples.

---

* No sugar! Serves 4.

Caramelized Bananas*

INGREDIENTS:

1 cup sugar
⅓ cup water
¼ cup sesame seeds
4 large bananas (firm, not overripe)
2 tablespoons sifted cornstarch
2 tablespoons butter
ice water

1. Combine sugar and water in saucepan. Add seeds. Cook until thick and syrupy.
2. Meanwhile, peel bananas. Cut into 2-inch-long slices.
3. Dust them lightly with cornstarch.
4. Heat butter in wok and lightly brown bananas.
5. To serve, have *ice* water, *hot bubbling* syrup, and bananas in a line. Dip bananas in syrup, then plunge immediately into ice water.
6. The syrup will immediately harden. Place on wax paper on cookie sheet.
7. Serve on toothpicks.

---

*Serves 4.

Cognac Berries*

INGREDIENTS:

1 cup blueberries, raspberries, or strawberries (sliced)
1 teaspoon cognac
½ cup sifted fiour
7 teaspoons sugar
⅛ cup milk
3 tablespoons sweet sherry
1 egg, beaten
4 cups oil for deep frying
¼ cup confectioner's sugar
½ teaspoon cinnamon

1. Sprinkle berries with cognac and let stand covered ½ hour.
2. Drain well.
3. Sift flour and sugar together.
4. Add milk, sherry, and egg, beating till very smooth.
5. Add berries. Coat well.
6. Heat 4 cups oil for deep frying in wok to 370°F.
7. Drop batter by the teaspoon into hot oil a few at a time.
8. Fry till golden. Drain on paper towels.
9. Sprinkle with mixture of cinnamon and confectioner's sugar.

*Serves 4.

Fried Bananas*

INGREDIENTS:

2 bananas (firm, not overripe)
3 tablespoons rum
1 cup oil
1 egg
¼ cup bread crumbs

1. Peel bananas, cut into 2-inch pieces and soak in rum for 30 minutes.
2. Heat oil in wok.
3. Meanwhile beat egg.
4. Dip banana in egg, then roll in bread crumbs.
5. Fry till golden brown.

*No sugar! Serves 4.

Apple Puffs*

INGREDIENTS:

1 cup flour
tiny pinch salt
1 teaspoon baking powder
3 tart apples
¼ teaspoon cinnamon
2 teaspoons coconut
2 tablespoons raisins
1 egg
1 cup milk
2 cups oil for cooking
honey
1 lemon, in wedges

1. Sift flour with salt and baking powder.
2. Core, peel and chop apples; sprinkle apples with cinnamon, coconut, and raisins.
3. Add to flour and mix with egg and milk to form batter.
4. Heat 2 cups oil in wok.
5. Drop by the teaspoon into hot oil.
6. Drain on paper towels.
7. Drizzle with honey and serve hot with wedges of lemon.

Note: For a gold star variation . . . serve Apple Puffs around a scoop of ice cream. It tastes just like warm apple pie a la mode!

*Serves 6. No sugar!

Old-Fashioned Steamed Carrot Pudding*

INGREDIENTS:

oil for mold
1½ cups all-purpose flour
1½ teaspoons baking soda
1½ cups sugar
¾ teaspoon salt
1½ teaspoons cloves
1½ teaspoons cinnamon
1½ teaspoons nutmeg
3 tablespoons butter or margarine, melted
3 eggs, well beaten
1½ cups raw carrots, grated
1½ raw potatoes, grated
1½ cups golden raisins
1 teaspoon wheat germ
boiling water

1. Thoroughly oil 6-cup mold.
2. Sift flour with soda, sugar, salt, and spices. Set aside.
3. Slowly stir butter into eggs in large bowl.
4. Stir in flour mixture and all remaining ingredients except water. Stir well.
5. Turn into prepared mold. Cover mold securely with aluminum foil. Then tent with aluminum foil and cover with wok lid.
6. Place on steam rack in wok.
7. Pour in boiling water to cover halfway up side of mold. Cover wok.
8. Steam 2 hours.
9. Remove mold from wok. Cool to lukewarm, then remove from mold. Serve warm.

Note: To store: cool pudding, completely wrap in aluminum foil. To serve: unwrap and steam 30 minutes till heated through.

---

*Serves 8 to 10.

Flaming Honey Rum Bananas*

Flaming and outrageously good . . . serve by themselves or over ice cream.

INGREDIENTS:

1 whole banana per serving
3 tablespoons butter
¼ cup honey
½ teaspoon cinnamon
¼ teaspoon nutmeg
1 miniature white rum (1/10 pint)
ice cream

1. Peel bananas. Slice lengthwise and in half.
2. Melt butter in wok.
3. Stir in honey and let sizzle.
4. Add bananas. Stir to coat. Cook till tender.
5. Sprinkle with cinnamon and nutmeg.
6. Pour in rum.
7. Stand back and ignite the rum.
8. Flame will flare high. Be sure to use a long wooden match and stand back.
9. When flame dies out, lift bananas out and put over ice cream. Pour on sauce.

---

*No sugar!

Dear Friend,

You see, it *is* easy!

We just made breakfast, lunch, dinner, and dessert in one "funny-shaped," tremendous pan! Remember, these recipes are just a beginning for you and your wok. My aim here was to have you fall in love with your wok and all it can do. Hopefully, I've succeeded.

Thank you for coming along with me. I hope in some way to have brought you joyful moments.

Annette Annechild
Wokmaster